THE
BIG
BOOK
OF
SUMO

THE BIG BOOK OF SUMO

History

Practice

Ritual

Fight

MINA HALL

STONE BRIDGE PRESS
Berkeley, California

Acknowledgments

When I first sat down and decided to write this sumo book, I had no idea what an undertaking it would be. From start to finish, it took over three years to complete. It would not have been possible without the support and help of my family and friends. A big sumo-style *arigato* to:

The Hall Family, the Yokoi family, the Elfstrum family, and the Shioi family. Special thanks to my mom for pointers on the illustrations, photography, and endless translations. *Osewa ni narimashita!* To Ken for his patience, and to my late-night animal companions who kept me company when I stayed up into the morning hours writing: Moki, Hoku, and Mike.

To my friends for their encouragement and advice: Matsumoto Tomie, Yasuda Haruyuki, and Emiko, Dan Taro, Wajima Hiroshi, Karimata Kokichi, my Japanese "teacher" Ota Yoko, Nagasaki Masaru, the Ito family, Okuii Sadao, Naoe Satoshi, Morita Saori, Kaneko Yoko, Fukuda Hideko, Rose Thomas, Julie Thomas, Patrick Tom, Dr. Edgar Porter, Ray Kaneyama, Boyd Imai, Peter Goodman, the Stone Bridge Press staff, Fujimoto Nobuko, Kamiyama Isao and Sumiko, and the entire "Borsalino Staff." A special thanks to my Japan "parents," the Nakagawas, Norio and Hiroko; thank you for always letting me have a comfortable place to stay with a great pink *ofuro*. Thanks also for the up-to-date sumo information, video tapes, and my favorite *yakiniku teishoku!*

Mahalo to the Hawaii boys: Konishiki (Salevaa Atisanoe), Akebono (Chad Rowan), Musashimaru (Fiamalu Penitani), Koryu (Eric Gaspar), Sunahama (Tyler Hopkins), Nanfu (Kaleo Kekaoha), Yamato (Glen Kalima), Takamio (John Feleunga), Daiki (Percy Kitapapa), Ozora (Troy Talamatai). Also to the many oyakata, rikishi, gyoji, yobidashi, tokoyama, and other sumo staff members who were so kind and taught me so much.

Finally, thank you to my mom and dad, Kimiko and Drue, who gave me the best of two countries.

—M.H.

Published by
Stone Bridge Press
P.O. Box 8208
Berkeley, CA 94707
TEL 510-524-8732
FAX 510-524-8711
E-MAIL sbp@stonebridge.com

For correspondence, updates, and further information about this and other Stone Bridge Press books, contact Stone Bridge Press online at **www.stonebridge.com**.

Text, illustrations (except on pages 11–13, 46–47), and photographs copyright © 1997 by Mina Hall. "Sumo Boy" and derivative designs are protected under applicable law.

Cover design by Harrington Young, Berkeley, California.

Text design and layout by Peter Goodman.

Printed in the United States of America.

10 9 8 7 6 5 4 3 2 1

LIBRARY OF CONGRESS
CATALOGING-IN-PUBLICATION DATA

Hall, Mina.
    The big book of sumo: history, practice, ritual, fight / Mina Hall.
        p. cm.
    ISBN 1-880656-28-0 (paper)
    1. Sumo. 2. Sumo—History. I. Title
GV1197.H35 1997
796.812'5—dc21   97-5629
                                                   CIP

CONTENTS

Terminology

The Japanese refer to a sumo wrestler as *osumo-san*, *rikishi*, or *sumotori*. Should you ever have the opportunity to speak to a sumo wrestler, you can use any of these terms when addressing him, or the wrestler's name plus the suffix *-zeki*. The word *sekitori* is used for wrestlers who have reached the upper, professional divisions. When you speak to a highly ranked wrestler, you should address him by his rank (e.g., Yokozuna or Ozeki).

Throughout this book currency amounts are given in $U.S., based on the rough conversion rate of $1 equals ¥100. Measurements are given here in English units, although Japan generally weighs its wrestlers in kilograms (1 kg. = 2.2 lbs.).

Because the sumo world and its conventions are so traditional, we have decided to keep Japanese names in traditional Japanese order; that is, the family name precedes the given name. Ex-wrestler Takamiyama, for example (who is also the Hawaiian-born Jesse Kuhaulua), has legally taken the name Watanabe Daigoro; *Watanabe* is the family name.

Japanese words related to sumo are used throughout the text and are defined at first mention. See the section "Sumo Words" that begins on page 138 for brief explanations.

INTRODUCTION

Being half Japanese and exposed to Japanese culture at an early age really had nothing to do with my interest in sumo. In fact, it wasn't until I went off to college at the University of Hawaii that I actually discovered the sport.

Although Hawaii is an American state, its location in the middle of the Pacific Ocean leaves it open to many Asian influences. It is probably the only place in America where Japanese words such as *shoyu*, *bento*, and *zori* are part of the everyday language. Seeing this as a great opportunity to study my mother's culture and language, I became an International Communications major, specializing in Japan. It was a demanding curriculum, especially since, at the time, I was a scholarship athlete on the university tennis team. My Japanese study time had to be worked in around practice, matches, and long road trips.

I became absorbed in my major and interested in all things Japanese: history, art, literature, music, food, and so on—anything to help me understand the complex Japanese language and culture. I was basically a sponge, taking in almost every aspect of the culture except its sports. Although I am a great sports fan, Japanese sports were not that attractive to me, simply because the level of competition really couldn't be compared to American standards. I grew up watching the NBA, the World Series, the Super Bowl, and heavyweight championship fights. Anything less seemed like Little League to me.

Talk in Hawaii started to center around a local guy who was going up in the ranks in Japan as a sumo wrestler. Much of the talk was about his size rather than his strength. He was from Nanakuli and a former football player at University High School, just down the street from my university. His name was Salevaa Atisanoe, otherwise known in Japan as Konishiki (or, affectionately, Sale). He was making his mark as the heaviest sumo wrestler in history. His weight at the time: a mere 550 pounds.

Having a local boy make it big is big news in Hawaii. But when I first saw Konishiki, along with many of the other sumo wrestlers, I just couldn't imagine calling sumo a "sport." My image of a sport is an activity that physically fit, muscular athletes participate in. These extremely overweight men needed a diet, or a few Weight Watchers classes. To me, they looked more like elephants than athletes.

One day I was flipping through a Japanese magazine and came across a picture of a sharp, intense, muscular man that, to my surprise, happened to be a sumo wrestler. He appeared to be performing some kind of ritual dance, and he was wearing a big white rope around his waist. I had no clue as to what he was doing and I couldn't read the *kanji* characters to figure out his name. Disappointed, I phoned home and told of my new discovery to my mom. Although she had little interest in sumo, she immediately said that I must have found a picture of one of the greatest sumo wrestlers of all time. I asked how he could possibly be so great because he was so slender compared with all the other huge wrestlers. She only responded, "Because he is Chiyonofuji."

And that is how it all started.

"Chiyono-who?!"

When you see a picture of Chiyonofuji, all of your preconceptions about sumo wrestlers are instantly wiped out. Here is a man whose body looks like it was chiseled out of marble, a husky version of a Michelangelo statue. His handsome face is highlighted by his sharp features and intense eyes (hence his nickname, "The Wolf"). I never thought I could feel this way about a sumo wrestler, but Chiyonofuji truly was beautiful.

Wanting to understand more about this wrestler and his mysterious sport, I read anything about sumo I could get my hands on. Unfortunately, at the time, outside of a few books, there really wasn't much information in English. So my main source of information became the Japanese television show "Sumo Digest," which was only a thirty-minute highlight show of the daily tournament matches.

After I returned home to Las Vegas from Hawaii for Christmas break in 1991, my mom showed me an article from a Japanese magazine. There was a picture of Chiyonofuji wearing a *haori-hakama* (formal Japanese wear) and wiping his eyes. Chiyonofuji had been defeated by a seventeen-year-old wrestler named Takahanada (today known as Yokozuna—Grand Champion—Takanohana) and thus had decided to retire with thirty-one championships, only one short of the record held by the great Taiho. How could he retire, I wondered? Why doesn't he go for the record? He was not that old, and he was still a very strong and respected yokozuna. Only one bad tournament and then he calls it quits? My mom replied, "Mina, that is the pride of a yokozuna. He cannot lose."

After graduating from the University of Hawaii in 1992, I was offered a job as a tennis coach at a sports club in Yokohama. Because I had always wanted to live in the country I had been studying for the past four years, I immediately took the offer. Teaching tennis in Japan is another book in itself, but I had a lot of fun. While I was there, a historic event was featured on all the Japanese television stations and in every magazine. A young American man from Hawaii had earned a spot at the top

Banner portrait of Chiyonofuji, hanging at the Kokugikan sumo arena, Tokyo.

of the sumo world. His name was Chad Rowan, or Akebono as he is known in Japan, and he had been promoted to yokozuna. A ceremony was held at Meiji Shrine in Tokyo, where he was to be officially invested with the rank in the presence of the gods. As Akebono made his entrance to the shrine, it started to snow. Even though I was wearing a heavy coat and muffler, I was shivering as I crawled my way in between thousands of people to watch. Although Akebono later told me that he was too nervous to think about being cold, he looked like he was freezing because he was barefoot and practically naked, wearing only a decorative apron and his yokozuna belt.

Akebono performed his first ritual ring-entering ceremony and every snowflake that hit his massive body instantly melted. He looked so dignified. As I watched him, I could only think about how neat it would be to talk to him, even if for only a few minutes. I wondered how this local boy from Hawaii had made it to the top of the traditional sport of Japan.

On my way home, I stopped by the local department store and went directly to the book section. I found a book on sumo with maps to all of the stables. A light bulb went on in my head. This is my ticket to the stables! I was a step closer to talking with Akebono. The only problem was that the book was written completely in Japanese and I couldn't read enough of the *kanji* characters to figure out which train station to get off at. A coworker at the tennis club helped translate the maps and showed me the route to take. While she was writing, she said, "Mina, you are crazy. Even if you know how to get there, they will never let you in. The sumo stables are very strict. Unless you have a connection or know someone who can intro-

8

duce you, it's impossible to talk to a wrestler." I almost gave up when I heard this. I could tell that living in Japan among millions of Japanese had begun to rub off on me. I was becoming like them: submissive, unwilling to take risks, and obeying all of the rules. But I was born in Las Vegas. I could feel that gambling blood start to rush to my head. The rational side of my brain told me to play the odds and percentages (which were definitely not in my favor). But the other side said to go for it and gamble! I knew that at least I had to try.

On my next day off, I went to Azumazeki-beya (the suffix -*beya* indicates a "stable" for training sumo wrestlers) in the hope of meeting the new yokozuna, Akebono. With my trusty map in hand, I boarded the early train from Yokohama to Ryogoku in eastern Tokyo. I completely forgot about the rush-hour crowds, so by the time I arrived at the stable and regained my respiration from the crushed-sardine-can train ride, practice was over. The lights were off and no one was around. I had traveled all the way to Ryogoku, only to arrive too late! Disappointed, I started to head back home when out of the corner of my eye I noticed that a door was open. Another light bulb went on! Thinking no one was around, I tiptoed my way in and started looking about. There was a huge portrait of the Hawaiian Jesse Kuhaulua when he won the 1972 Nagoya tournament and a statue of his bust. The doors to the *dohyo* (the wrestling ring) were also open. It was the first time I had seen the ring up close.

I thought I was doing a pretty good spy imitation when all of a sudden someone from behind called out in Japanese in a deep, echoing voice: "What can I do for you?" My heart started racing. Caught! I turned around and through the shadows could see a young, but very big sumo wrestler. I thought he would call the police or maybe just push me out the door himself. I didn't know what to say or do, so I just looked at him. He asked again, "What can I do for you? Do you understand Japa-

One-time juryo wrestler Goken, enjoying a book.

nese?" I understood him, I just didn't know what to say. Panicking, I told him I wanted to see Akebono. (What a thing to say, having just been caught sneaking around the stable!) The sumo wrestler asked, "Does he know you? Are you a friend?" Very softly, I told him that I didn't know Akebono, but that I was from Hawaii too. Somehow, that just didn't seem to be enough. Off the top of my head I added, "I, uh, . . . uh . . . I work for the newspaper there and I uh . . . well, if it's possible, I . . . uh . . . want to do an interview with Akebono."

I was so nervous, I thought that surely he could tell I was making up the story. But he politely told me, "Oh, I see. I'm sorry, but Yokozuna is not here right now. Because he just got promoted, he's very busy. If you come back tomorrow morning, I'll tell him that you stopped by. What was your name?" Suddenly my nervousness went away and I felt like a reporter. I told him my name and as I walked out I said, *"Domo. Mata ashita. . . . Yoroshiku onegaishimasu!"* (Thanks, and I'll see you tomorrow!).

The next day, as the young wrestler promised, Akebono was there. After he practiced, ate lunch, and had his hair done, I finally got to talk to him. The first thing I said was, "Chad, thanks for talking to me. But I have to tell you something. . . . I'm not really a reporter. I just wanted to talk with you." He laughed and said that that was the first time anyone had made up such a good, convincing story. He said he didn't have any plans for the afternoon, so he didn't mind. We talked for over an hour about all kinds of things: sumo, Hawaii, life in Japan, food, music, and so on. I was a stranger to him, but he treated me like an old high school friend. (Incidentally, after my first meeting with him, my story *was* published in the *Honolulu Advertiser*.)

Now I really wanted to learn more about sumo and understand all of its rituals and traditions. I was amazed at how well Akebono had adjusted to sumo's strict, disciplined lifestyle. He once told me that when a foreign wrestler comes to Japan, he must completely start over. He explained, "When I came over here, I completely forgot everything that I learned in my first eighteen years of life in Hawaii. I couldn't come over here thinking that I'm the big American, and I'll show them how it's done. Sumo is their sport. It's been around for over two thousand years and it's not going to change. I knew that I would have to be the one to change."

From that moment on, I was hooked. Akebono had opened my eyes and guided me through the door to a whole new world.

On my days off, I was a regular visitor to the stable. I became friends with some of the wrestlers and with the stable manager. I ate *chankonabe* (sumo stew) with Akebono and the okamisan (stablemaster's wife), watched him give countless photo sessions and interviews in English and Japanese, observed his stablemates making his yokozuna belt, and even received a free pass to a Tokyo tournament. Sometimes, when his mom sent food from Hawaii, Akebono would save a little for me. Because you can't buy Hawaiian food in Japan, I really appreciated his thoughtfulness. Akebono, along with everyone else in the stable, was unbelievably nice to me. Eventually, I branched out and went to Takasago-beya to talk with Konishiki and the other Hawaiian wrestlers, to Musashigawa-beya to hang out with Musashimaru, and even to a few stables with no foreign wrestlers. The rikishi themselves are physically huge, yet they have so much grace and dignity. They can be so fierce and violent in the ring, and yet so gentle and soft out of it. They radiate an inner strength that is hard to describe . . . you just have to feel it.

The more I learned about sumo, the more I enjoyed it. The beauty of the sport overwhelmed me. It is a simple contest with no equipment involved. There are no balls, no goals, no baskets, no bats, no rackets, no padding, and no teammates. It is only man against man. It is the ultimate test of power, technique, and concentration. It is sport in its purest form. So pure that it almost surpasses the boundaries of sport and reaches the borders of art. Without speaking, using only eye contact and instinct, wrestlers synchronize their moves and perform their rituals together. Some wrestlers are so skilled that during the warm-up period they can even synchronize their breathing. There is an aura in the ring as they focus all of their energy to defeat one another. Yet, before the match and after, whether a wrestler has won or lost, without expressing any emotions, he must lower his head and bow. All sumo matches begin and end with this gesture of respect.

My time in Japan was a great learning experience. I actually saw up close what most foreigners or even Japanese would never have the chance to see. I was inside the closed world of sumo. This book is what I have learned from my time spent with its wrestlers. Although I also did research by watching numerous television programs, going to tournaments, and reading books and magazines, the bulk of the information here comes directly from the wrestlers, coaches, and hairdressers. I hope *The Big Book of Sumo* becomes your key to understanding the fascinating ancient national sport of Japan.

A BRIEF HISTORY OF SUMO

What exactly is sumo? Man versus man, in a test of strength, is one of civilization's oldest contests. All over the world—in Egypt, Mongolia, China, Indonesia, and in other parts of Asia, Africa, and Europe—there is historical evidence that a form of wrestling existed. Sumo is Japan's national sport and involves many ancient rituals. Its history is rich and long. According to Japanese legend, as described in the ancient chronicle *Kojiki* (Record of Ancient Matters), the fate of the Japanese islands once rested upon the outcome of a sumo bout between two gods, Takemikazuchi and Takeminakata. Takemikazuchi emerged victorious and thus determined who would rule the land. A shrine in Shimane Prefecture today marks the site of that first sumo match.

Legend aside, the sport of sumo dates back some fifteen hundred years. Its origins were religious, based on Shinto rituals. Matches were held at Shinto shrines and dedicated to the gods in hopes of good harvests. The bouts took place along with music, poetry reading, sacred dancing, and drama.

During the Nara (645–794) and Heian (794-1185) periods, sumo known as *sechie-zumo* was ceremonially performed once a year on the seventh day of the seventh lunar month (early August) at the imperial court in the presence of royalty. Court officials were always on the lookout for exceptionally strong men or skilled wrestlers who could participate in the yearly event. During the Heian period, wrestlers who entered the ring from the right side wore an ornamental hair pin, made out of cotton and shaped like a *yugao no hana* (calabash). Those who entered from the left wore pins in the shape of an *aoi no hana* (hollyhock). The winner of the bout gave his ornament to the next rikishi on his side, while the losing side would have to use a new one. (The term *hanamichi*, used today to identify the aisles that lead from the dressing rooms to the *dohyo*, comes from this practice.) A match official would stick an arrow in the ground for every wrestler who won a match. After all the bouts were completed, the arrows were counted to determine the winning side.

Early sumo was a combination of wrestling, boxing, and judo. Matches were quite violent and had few rules. During the Kamakura period (1185–1334), a military dictatorship or shogunate was established and bloody wars were fought throughout Japan. It was at this time that sumo was implemented as part of the military's training program. Many of the wrestling techniques practiced were used to force an enemy down to the ground where he could easily be apprehended. Jujitsu developed from this.

The powerful warlord Oda Nobunaga (1534–82) was a great sumo enthusiast and organized several tournaments at his castle. At one tournament in February of 1578 over fifteen hundred wrestlers gathered to take part in the competition. It was at this tournament that a circle boundary to designate the wrestling ring was drawn for the first time. Nobunaga's successor, Toyotomi Hideyoshi (1537–98), also en-

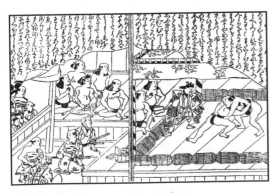

Old print showing a square sumo ring.

joyed sumo and once arranged a match between two top wrestlers, Irie Okuranosuke and Toku Inosuke. He was so impressed by the pure power of the two rikishi that he stopped the match before a winner could be decided. Hideyoshi's nephew, Hidetsugu, kept over a hundred wrestlers among his personal warriors. He would occasionally have them put on exhibitions for his viewing pleasure.

The civil wars of Japan finally ended in 1603 when Tokugawa Ieyasu became shogun and united the entire country under his rule. Over the next 250 years the land was mostly at peace, and samurai warriors, who had no way of venting their aggression, were encouraged to turn their fighting skills into disciplined art forms. Samurai who studied kendo, sumo, and other martial arts lived a strict life following the code of Bushido ("the way of the warrior"), which emphasized loyalty, honor, determination, humility, respect to a master, and fulfilling one's obligations.

During this time, "street sumo" was also very popular. Men would challenge each other as crowds gathered to watch and cheer for their favorite fighters. The winner of a bout was the wrestler who threw his opponent down to the ground or into the crowd. But because the fighting was so violent, it was often difficult to clearly determine the winner. Arguments broke out, forcing the authorities to intervene. The Tokugawa shogunate banned street sumo and passed a new law that permitted sumo only for the benefit of the gods. The resulting matches were called *kanjin-zumo* (benefit sumo) and were used to raise money for the construction of new temples and shrines and for the repairing of old ones. Tournament promoters, some of whom were *ronin* (masterless samurai)

Old-style print of a yokozuna performing the ring-entering ceremony.

or former wrestlers, were required to obtain special permission from a temple in order to hold a tournament. These promoters, who came to be known as *toshiyori*, or elders, thus acted as liaisons between the government and temple officials and the wrestlers. They were responsible for staging the events, as well as for preventing arguments and fighting. The elders also began setting up areas where young wrestlers could be trained.

During *kanjin-zumo*, large rice bags were placed on the ground to make a circular barrier. Later, four poles were placed in the corners and a roof was placed overhead to delineate the official fighting area. Tournaments were held twice a year and for only ten days. However, they could sometimes take up to three months to complete due to bad weather or political circumstances within the shogunate. Eventually, retired wrestlers formed the Sumo Kaisho, today known as the Nihon Sumo Kyokai (Japan Sumo Association), and began organizing the tournaments.

Sumo's popularity was mainly concentrated in Kyoto and Osaka and did not extend to Edo (where the shogunate was located; in 1868 the city's name was changed to Tokyo). It wasn't until the strong rivals Tanikaze (an Edo native) and Onogawa emerged that sumo developed a following in Edo. Huge crowds would come out to watch these two wrestlers battle. Women, who at the time were not allowed to watch official tournaments, would gather around the practice areas and throw their *haori* (jacket) or *obi* (sash) to them.

Gradually, the Sumo Association of Edo became dominant in Japan. Young wrestlers from all over the country would travel to Edo to train. Feudal lords sponsored exceptionally strong wrestlers. A wrestler that was so honored was given a *kesho-mawashi* (ceremonial apron) with the lord's family crest printed on it, a large allowance, and samurai status if he did not already come from a warrior background. Wrestlers participated in tournaments and were ranked accordingly on a *banzuke* (ranking sheet). For a short time, a square-shaped ring was used for bouts, but it was quickly done away with in favor of the circle. Sumo stables were organized, rules were laid out, and professional sumo emerged, not only as a performance for the gods and feudal lords but also as entertainment for the common people of Japan. The sport prospered and, along with going to Kabuki and to Yoshiwara (the brothel district), it became one of the top forms of entertainment in Edo.

In 1789, Yoshida Oikaze, a referee from Kumamoto, established himself as the chief representative of the sumo world. He gained the shogun's support and was in charge of the licensing of all referees and yokozuna. Yoshida, along with Edo's Sumo Association elders, developed rules for a series of purification rituals that were to be performed prior to the matches. He introduced the *yokozuna menkyo* (grand champion license) and issued the first two to Tanikaze and Onogawa. (To this day, newly promoted yokozuna still receive their yokozuna license from a descendant of the Yoshida family.) Ten days later, Tanikaze became the first yokozuna to perform the *dohyo-iri* (ring-entering ceremony) while wearing the *yokozuna tsuna* (yokozuna belt). At this time, however, yokozuna was not an official rank (the highest rank was ozeki). Having a yokozuna license only certified that a champion wrestler could perform the *dohyo-iri*. The first yokozuna to be listed on a *banzuke* was Nishinoumi in 1890, and it was not until 1909 that the rank of yokozuna was officially established.

From October 1833 until 1907, sumo was regularly held outdoors at Ryogoku Ekoin in eastern Tokyo, the first permanent site for sumo tournaments. On the morning of a tournament a large drum was beaten to announce the event. Workers would also walk through neighborhoods pounding drums and encouraging people to attend the matches (a practice that continues even today).

Sumo wrestlers were among the first Japanese to greet the American responsible for opening the doors of trade with Japan. From the early seventeenth century, Japan had been a closed country, barring any foreign influence. Japanese were not permitted to leave the country and foreigners were not allowed in (except for a few traders around Nagasaki). Commodore Matthew Perry of the United States arrived in Yokohama in February 1854 and successfully negotiated a treaty to begin trade with Japan. Japanese officials, as a friendly gesture of goodwill, gave the Americans many gifts, including some two hundred large bags of rice. The bags were so heavy, around 135 pounds each, that the sailors could not carry them to the ships. Puzzled, they waited, not knowing what to do. Then suddenly, out of nowhere, twenty-five sumo wrestlers appeared. Effortlessly, each one loaded two bags on his shoulders and carried the rice to the ship.

Following this, the American crew was invited to a sumo demonstration. Commodore Perry was surprised by the mammoth size of the wrestlers. In his personal journal written during the Japan expedition, he recorded his astonishment:

A sumo wrestler carrying a heavy bale of rice to Commodore Perry's ship.

Never have I seen grouped together so many brawny men, giving a better idea of an equal number of stall-fed bulls than human beings. . . . One of them was especially brought to me that I might examine his massive form; massive because his frame was covered with a mass of flesh, which to our ideas of athletic qualities would seem to incapacitate him from any violent exercise. . . . [He was] entirely naked, excepting the invariable strip of cloth round the loins. . . . Two whose names were called stepped into the ring and began to eye each other with threatening looks, rather dramatic to be sure, stamping the soft ground with their naked feet, stooping down and grasping handfuls of the earth with which they rubbed themselves under the arm pits, and seemed to besmear the palms of their hands. Whether this was to imitate the action of the bull, who paws the earth when preparing for an attack, or for what purpose, I am ignorant, but it seemed to be very foolish.*

However unimpressed, Commodore Perry and his men thus were probably the first group of foreigners ever to witness a sumo match.

Although sumo is traditionally considered a male sport (women are not even allowed to touch the *dohyo*), *onna-zumo* or women's sumo existed in the 1700s. It started in Osaka and was performed in connection with houses of prostitution. The matches pitted women against women and women against blind men. By 1744, *onna-zumo*'s popularity had reached Edo. Tournaments were held at Asakusa Temple until authorities declared them immoral and closed them down. However, due to popular demand, the matches continued, now at different locations in northern Japan. Unfortunately for the women involved (some of whom were actually skilled wrestlers), from the beginning *onna-zumo* was controversial, and by 1926 it was completely banned.

Not long after Commodore Perry's visit to Japan, the Tokugawa shogunate

*Cited in *The Japan Expedition, 1852–1854: The Personal Journal of Commodore Matthew C. Perry*. Roger Pineau, ed. Washington, D.C.: Smithsonian University Press, 1968.

began to fall apart. In 1868, Emperor Meiji was restored to the throne. The Japanese realized that after centuries of being a closed country, they needed to catch up with the rest of the world. Many people put away their kimono and began wearing Western clothes. Men were no longer allowed to carry swords and were ordered to cut off their *chonmage* (topknots) in favor of short, Western hair styles. An exception, however, was made for sumo wrestlers, who were able to keep their *chonmage* because it served as a head protector in case of a fall during a bout. But in time the public started to view sumo as "too barbaric" and "too old-fashioned." Attendance at sumo tournaments started to fall, causing a crisis for the Sumo Association. Wrestlers, without the extra financial support of feudal lords (whose fortunes had been greatly reduced after the Meiji Restoration), found themselves in a terrible situation. During this troubled time, a ranked wrestler, Takasago Uragoro, rebelled against the main sumo association and founded a rival group of his own.

Desperately trying to improve their image, rikishi began doing public service. They assisted fire departments, helped build temples and memorials, and even carried banners for the imperial family during processions. The Sumo Association itself underwent major reform, changing its name from Sumo Kaisho to Tokyo Ozumo Kyokai (Tokyo Grand Sumo Association). Directors were elected, wrestler's wages were set, and the final authority of bouts went from the gyoji (referee) to the ringside shinpan (judges). By 1872, women were allowed to watch official tournaments. Influential government officials began to voice their approval of the sport. The major change in public attitude, however, took place after Emperor Meiji attended a sumo demonstration. With the emperor's strong support as well as the great performances of the yokozuna Umegatani and Nishinoumi, sumo survived the Meiji Restoration and went on to become the national sport of Japan. Instead of feudal lords, it was now politicians and captains of industry who sponsored and rooted for sumotori.

In 1909, the Kokugikan (National Sumo Stadium) was built in Honjo Ekoin Keidai. The publisher *Jiji Shinpo-sha* began the custom of presenting the champion wrestler with a portrait of himself and a flag to the winning team. Later, in 1925, in front of the royal prince (who would soon become Emperor Hirohito), sumo was performed at the Imperial Palace, and a cup was awarded to tournament champions in the prince's name; this trophy is known today as the Tenno-hai (Emperor's Cup). Soon after, with the encouragement of the Imperial Palace, the Osaka and Tokyo sumo associations merged to form the Dai Nihon Ozumo Kyokai (All-Japan Grand Sumo Association).

Four official tournaments—in January, March, May, and September—were established in 1927. In 1928, live radio broadcasting of sumo tournaments started and time limits were set for the warm-up periods (before then, rikishi would start a match only after both wrestlers felt ready). The upper makuuchi division was allowed ten minutes to warm up, the juryo divisions seven, and the makushita and lower divisions only five.

In the 1930s emerged one of the greatest wrestlers of all time, Yokozuna Futabayama of Tatsunami-beya, who went on to win twelve tournament championships and set the record that still stands today for most consecutive wins (sixty-nine). A legendary superstar, Futabayama kept it a secret until after his retirement that he was blind in one eye. While he was still a yokozuna, Futabayama opened up his own stable (a practice no longer allowed) and called it Futabayama Dojo; the name was later changed to Tokitsukaze-beya. Futabayama's commanding presence took sumo to an unprecedented height of popularity. In elementary schools, sumo became a required subject for boys' physical education classes. Sumo tournaments were also extended from ten days to thirteen in 1937, and then to fifteen in 1939.

Other Dates in Sumo History

1950s	rival yokozuna Tochinishiki and Wakanohana I
1958	the new schedule of six tournaments a year is established
1960s	rival yokozuna Kashiwado and Taiho
1965	the rule is established that only rikishi from the same stable do not fight against each other
1969	instant replay starts for disputed makuuchi matches
1970s	rival yokozuna Tamanoumi and Kitanofuji
1972	Takamiyama becomes the first foreigner to win a championship
1975–	rival yokozuna Wajima and Kitanoumi
1981	Chiyonofuji is yokozuna
1985	the new Kokugikan is constructed in Ryogoku
1987	Konishiki becomes first foreign ozeki
1993	Akebono becomes the first foreign yokozuna
1994	Takanohana is yokozuna

The sumo boom had to take a back seat to war in the 1940s. Many young wrestlers were drafted into the army, and several stables were destroyed by fire bombing. Although the Kokugikan was used by the military as a bomb factory and thus was unavailable for tournaments, a few sumo matches were held at local parks, sometimes even on baseball fields.

After World War II, a defeated Japan was ruled by the Allied Occupation forces. The foreign troops took over the Kokugikan and renamed it Memorial Hall. They installed an ice skating rink and offices for the soldiers inside the arena. Tournaments were canceled, but in 1947 a match was held at the outer gardens of Meiji Shrine in western Tokyo. Tournaments continued there for the next two years. In 1950, a new Kokugikan in Kuramae was constructed. It became the home of sumo for the next thirty-four years. In 1953, live television broadcasting started and sumo's popularity rose again. In 1957 a school for sumo recruits was created, and many reforms in the organization of professional sumo were instituted. A November tournament was added in 1957 and a July tournament in 1958, for a total of six main tournaments each year. In 1985 a new Kokugikan was built in Ryogoku, just across the Sumida River in northeastern Tokyo.

Today, making it to the top of professional sumo is a huge endeavor. All wrestlers start at the same bottom rung on the ladder and must slowly work their way up. It doesn't matter who you are or who you know. In sumo, only results can bring you respect. As Akebono says, "You either make it, or you die, or you go home."

The rules of sumo are simple. Two wrestlers enter the circular *dohyo* (ring) wearing nothing except a *mawashi* (a narrow belt that passes beneath the legs and around the waist). A wrestler wins by driving his opponent out of the ring or by forcing any part of his body, other than the soles of his feet, to touch the ground. This can be done by pushing, slapping, arm throws, leg trips, or any combination of the seventy established techniques. Hair pulling, striking with a closed fist, choking, poking the eyes, kicking in the stomach or chest, and grabbing in the groin area are prohibited.

Before the match begins, wrestlers perform a sequence of meaningful rituals. Then, as anticipation of the match builds, the wrestlers concentrate and focus their energy toward the explosive *tachiai*, or initial clash. Matches are usually over within a matter of seconds, although a long match can last several minutes. The bouts are a demonstration of a wrestler's sheer strength or clever technique. Because there are no height or weight restrictions, some of the most interesting matches occur when a smaller wrestler is matched against an opponent twice his size.

Despite modern times and technology, sumo has preserved the traditions of yesterday. The sumo rituals and ceremonies that took place before Commodore Perry and his men remain substantially unchanged to this day. The wrestlers compete in traditional ways and must live a rigid, hierarchical lifestyle. Unlike baseball or football players, who can practice or play a game and then go home to a normal life, sumo wrestlers are sumo wrestlers twenty-four hours a day, 365 days a year. A wrestler's behavior, the clothes he wears, and every ritual he performs all have their roots in the past. Strong wrestlers were once awarded samurai status. Today, yokozuna, sumo's grand champions, are treated with awe and respect by the media, by politicians, by their fellow wrestlers, and by their adoring fans.

The participants in Japan's sacred national sport, however, are no longer purely Japanese. Like many other sports in Japan, such as baseball and soccer, sumo has come to be influenced by foreign athletes. Sixty years ago, Shoji Hiraga, a Japanese-American, became the first foreigner ever to be listed on the *banzuke* (there were several Koreans in sumo before him, but because Korea was a colony of Imperial Japan, they were not considered "foreign"). At first, many Japanese thought that foreigners in sumo were amusing, like a sideshow at a circus. They believed a foreigner could never make it to the top of their disciplined and traditional sport. Only a Japanese could possess the necessary strength and *hinkaku* (dignity) to become a yokozuna.

Japanese complacency immediately started to change once the foreigners began winning tournaments. Several wrestlers from Hawaii, in particular, have had a great impact and burst to the forefront of the sumo world. Japan's xenophobic response to the foreign "threat" has led to the establishment of an unwritten quota of two foreign wrestlers per stable.

But whether a wrestler is a *gaijin* (foreigner) or a *nihonjin* (Japanese), all sumotori are treated equally and must start at the bottom. It is a long, hard climb to reach the glory at the top, and the road begins at the stable.

THE RIKISHI ROAD

To become a sumo wrestler, one must first join a *heya,* or stable. Many hopefuls are recruited by the oyakata (stablemaster) or by scouts affiliated with the stable. Before a candidate is allowed official entrance, he must first satisfy the criteria laid out by the Sumo Association. That is, he must:

1. have completed junior high school

2. be between the ages of fifteen and twenty-two (collegiate sumo athletes are accepted until the age of twenty-five)

3. be at least 5'6" (there is no height requirement for established amateur and college sumotori)

4. weigh at least 165 pounds

5. have his parents' or guardian's consent

6. pass a standard physical

A non-Japanese candidate in addition must have two Japanese guarantors and a visa.

The physical exams—called *shindeshi kensa*—are given six times a year, once before every tournament. There have been cases of wrestlers going to extremes in order to pass the first stage. If a few pounds underweight, some have been known to stuff themselves full of rice, potatoes, and water just before the weigh-in, only to have the food come back up shortly after. Mainoumi, currently a

Stable entryway nameplates on this page, clockwise from top right: Taiho-beya, Takasago-beya, Kokonoe-beya, Futagoyama-beya.

maegashira wrestler, was just short of the minimum height requirement when he went for his exam. Desperate to become a professional wrestler, he obtained a silicone implant on the top of his head to give him the extra inches needed to pass! (He has since had it removed.) In 1994, after failing three times, another young hopeful named Harada Koji added 6 inches worth of silicone to his height, causing an uproar. He will be the last wrestler to add inches to his head, however, because the Sumo Association has since banned all silicone injections.

Once permitted entry, a wrestler is expected to train and live in his stable for the duration of his career. However, if he marries or reaches a high rank he is allowed to move out into his own place. There are no player trades in sumo as there are in other sports. Thus, the stable where a wrestler starts his career will be the one where he ends it.

New recruits must shave all facial hair and remove any tattoos, which are considered impure marks on the body. A few Hawaiian wrestlers have had their tattoos painfully burned off, leaving major scars. Many first-year wrestlers debut under their real names, while others are given a *shikona*, or fighting name. Novices are also required to attend a six-month school run by the Sumo Association in

Ryogoku. From 7 to 10 am, they practice together, under the watchful eyes of coaches, and learn the basic techniques of sumo. They also learn how to properly tie the *mawashi* (belt) and how to perform the many ceremonial and purification rituals. Following practice, the wrestlers gather in a classroom where they are taught the history of sumo, sports medicine, Japanese, poetry, calligraphy, and other general subjects. After eating lunch, the wrestlers return to their stables.

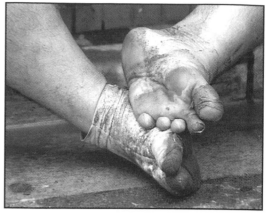

Because they practice barefoot everyday, sumo wrestlers' feet are very hard and callused. Pictured above are the feet of wrestler Musoyama—showing just how rough the rikishi road really is!

1.

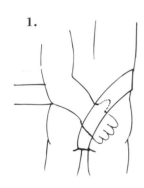

2.

MAWASHI FACTS

Length: about 30 feet

Width: about 2 feet

Weight: 8–11 pounds

Material: during practice, canvas; during tournaments, wrestlers in juryo division and above wear *mawashi* made of silk

Color: during practice, wrestlers in the makushita division and below wear black, and juryo and above wear white; during tournaments, rules stipulate that sekitori wear black, navy blue, or purple, but the influence of TV has led to other color choices for ranked wrestlers, including blue, red, yellow, orange, green, black, and purple

3.

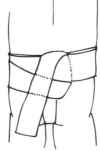

4.

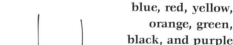
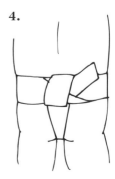

How you put on the *mawashi* can make a difference. Some wrestlers pull their *mawashi* so tightly across that it takes two attendants to put it on. They want the belt to be snug across their body so their opponent can't easily get a good grip on it. Others will put it on loosely so that even when their opponent jerks them, the slack in the belt will give their body time to catch up. Some even splash water on their *mawashi* to make it slippery— it is illegal, however, to put any kind of foreign substance (except for a minimum amount of water and sweat) on the *mawashi*.

PRACTICE

The training schedule rarely changes. The youngest and lowest-ranked wrestlers start practice first, usually around 4:30 or 5 o'clock in the morning. Wearing dark-colored cotton *mawashi*, they warm up in the *dohyo* by themselves until a coach or the stablemaster arrives.

Whenever a coach, oyakata, or higher-ranked wrestler enters, the younger wrestlers must offer a proper and respectful greeting. Around 8 am, the sekitori (wrestlers ranked in the juryo division or above) make their way down from their private rooms and join practice. Wearing white *mawashi*, they are very easy to rec-ognize. The lower-ranked wrestlers who are assigned to kitchen duty for the day then leave to begin their chores and to prepare lunch.

During practice, wrestlers take part in many exercises designed to increase flexibility and strength. Wrestlers will do the standard push-ups and sit-ups along with dozens of *shiko* (lifting the legs alternately as high as possible, then stomping them down, slapping the hands on the knees, and exhaling, ending in a crouched position). The *shiko* is the most basic sumo exercise, and wrestlers will sometimes do hundreds of them in a day. *Shiko* are also performed repeatedly during the rituals of a tournament.

Another leg strengthener, *suriashi*, is

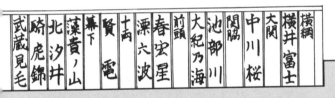

The Training Area

The training area (keikoba) is on the first floor of a stable. It is a room with wood-paneled walls, a dirt floor, and a dohyo *(ring) about 15 feet in diameter. Usually in the corner of the practice area are small weights and a* teppo, *or tall wooden pole, used for striking and pushing exercises. On one wall are posted the stable's rankings. Every wrestler's name is written in fancy calligraphy on a small wood-*

en board, and all the boards are arranged according to rank (the highest ranked person is on the far right and the lowest on the far left), as in the illustration at above left. Any referee or hairdresser that is affiliated with the stable will have his name similarly displayed, after the wrestlers.

On one side of the practice room is the agarizashiki, *or spectators viewing area. With a raised floor of either wood or tatami, it is where fans, sponsors, and the oyakata sit to observe the daily practice. Because the practice area is not equipped with air conditioning or heaters, there are usually several windows open for ventilation. The* dohyo *is considered sacred ground, so there is always a Shinto altar somewhere in the practice area.*

Some popular stables where practice can be viewed are listed on pages 120–22.

Shiko.

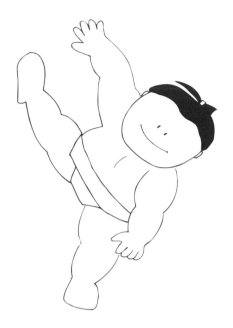

ground. This is very painful, and often wrestlers cannot do it alone. A partner will hold the legs apart or push down on the back.

A pushing exercise for the arms and shoulders is done against a tall wooden pole (*teppo*), usually found in the corner of the practice area. A wrestler faces the pole front on and strikes it with the palms of his hands. He alternates his arms and follows each strike by stepping with the same foot. (For example, if he strikes the pole with his right hand he will follow with his right foot.) Nowadays, many wrestlers also use weights as a part of their training.

done in a crouched position with the hands in front, bent at the elbows. The wrestler slides his feet forward, alternating legs, or jumps together with both legs, pushing with the arms and keeping the body low to the ground.

A common stretching exercise is *matawari*, or thigh splits. A wrestler sits with his legs as far apart as possible (almost in the splits) and then leans forward until his stomach touches the

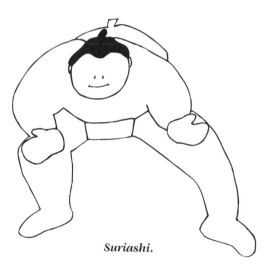

Suriashi.

Matawari.

Teppo (pushing exercise).

After warming up, rikishi take part in challenge matches. These are similar to the competitive matches seen on television, without all of the rituals and preparation time. The winner, who picks his next opponent, continues to fight until he is defeated. It is at this time that lower-ranked wrestlers may be given the chance to fight against higher-ranked ones. As a means of stamina training, two wrestlers can challenge each other for a series of matches (*sanban-geiko*). After a while, lower-ranked wrestlers must stand aside as the higher-ranked rikishi (the sekitori, or wrestlers ranked juryo or above) begin to practice against each other.

During practice it is very easy to distinguish the sekitori from the other wrestlers. Not only is the color of their *ma-washi* different, but they are the ones giving orders and basically running the practice along with the oyakata. Part of a sekitori's job is to help train and push the lower-ranked wrestlers. The apprentices, in return for the sekitori's advice, respectfully act as his servants, continuously wiping him down, offering him water, and holding the salt, which is thrown onto the *dohyo* for purification. As Akebono explains, "If you want to understand sumo, you should watch the practice instead of the tournaments. In practice you can see what a difference ranking makes. It is what sumo life is based on."

Near the end of practice, wrestlers

The average number of wrestlers in a stable is about fifteen. The smallest stable has two; the largest has almost fifty! During tournaments, wrestlers do a light workout from about 8 until 10 am. They shower, eat lunch, and then relax upstairs by watching TV or taking a nap. They get their hair done and then head to the arena a couple hours before they enter the ring.

Challenge match.

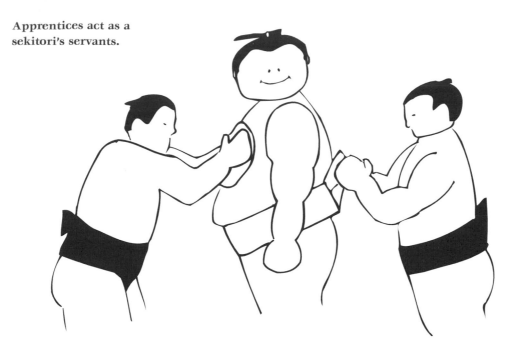

Apprentices act as a sekitori's servants.

take part in *butsukari-geiko*, in which one wrestler runs into another and pushes him to the edge of the *dohyo*. The defender, while yelling, tries to hold the attacker as he slides backward toward the edge. Oftentimes he will throw him down so the attacker can practice falling. After only a couple of minutes, the attacker becomes exhausted. If he cannot get up after being thrown, the other ranked wrestlers or a coach will kick him and scold him to continue. Sometimes, this drill appears to be more a form of punishment or harassment. But some argue it is done to devel-

Butsukari-geiko.

A former makushita wrestler, who never made the salaried ranks, was once asked whether—if he could go back in time and start over in sumo, knowing he would have to go through all of the hardships and not reach the top level—he would enter the sumo world again. Without hesitation he replied, "Yes, because sumo isn't just about becoming number one. Being a rikishi has taught me about sacrifice, hard work, respecting my elders, and carrying myself with dignity. When I entered sumo, I was only a child. But now as I leave, I am a man."

Jog-shuffling around the *dohyo* after practice.

op strong character and to teach a wrestler that no matter how many times he falls, he must get up and continue to fight.

After the matches and drills are completed, the wrestlers will line up around the *dohyo* with their knees bent, holding the belt of the person directly in front. They slowly jog-shuffle around the *dohyo* while chanting, *"Yoisho, yoisho, yoisho!"* Their feet do not leave the ground. Sometimes a coach or sekitori will hold out a bamboo stick that forces the wrestlers to crouch down to pass under it. This is a great leg strengthener.

Practice generally ends with stretching exercises and with *sonkyo*, which is breathing deeply, almost in a meditative state, while squatting down with a straight back and hands placed on the knees. Practice is usually over about 11 am.

Following practice, lower-ranked wrestlers clean the training area. After sweeping and watering the *dohyo*, they

throw salt onto the ring to purify it; a Shinto *gohei*, a small wooden stick with white paper folded around it, may be placed upright in the middle of the ring to sym-

Sonkyo.

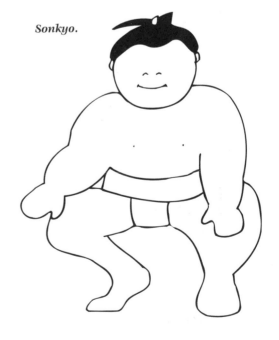

23

ETIQUETTE FOR VIEWING PRACTICE

Most people aren't aware that almost anyone interested can watch a morning practice session without charge—considering the high price of tournament tickets, this is a real bargain. The open-door policy of most stables permits a limited number of fans to watch from the *agarizashiki*, or viewing area. Reservations are not necessary, but you might want to call just to make sure that the wrestlers are in town and a practice is scheduled. (Usually no practices are held the week after a tournament, and wrestlers are often on road trips performing exhibitions.) When a tournament is nearing, strong sekitori (the higher-ranked wrestlers) regularly go to other stables for practice, a custom called *degeiko*.

Because so many popular sekitori may be gathered at one place during *degeiko*, these practices are often closed to the public. If you want to catch a star sekitori in action, you should therefore try to go to his stable at least one week before a tournament begins. Arrive early, before 9 am; if the viewing area becomes too crowded the front doors will be locked and no additional guests will be allowed in. Some stables do not allow visitors during tournaments. Others, like Futagoyama-beya (home of Takanohana and Wakanohana), do not let anyone in at any time except invited guests and members of the press. (See pages 120–22 for a listing of stables and their addresses and phone numbers; be prepared to make all visiting arrangements in Japanese.)

1. When entering and leaving, bow toward the oyakata as a sign of respect and gratitude for allowing you into his stable.

2. Remove your shoes before entering the viewing area.

3. Sit quietly and refrain from talking too much.

4. Sumo is a traditional, male sport. Women should wear pants instead of skirts and sit Japanese style, with the legs folded under or to the side. Sitting cross-legged is not recommended, but if you are unable to sit Japanese style for more than a minute or so, don't worry about it. You're a foreigner and will be forgiven.

5. Do not bring in food and drinks.

6. Do not go too close to the *dohyo* or talk to a wrestler during practice.

7. Unless a coach or wrestler specifically tells you not to take pictures, photographs are generally allowed. The practice area is not well lit, but you shouldn't use flash, as it disturbs the wrestlers' concentration. Try a high-speed film (ASA 400 +).

8. Do not touch the *dohyo*, even after practice is over.

9. If you want to get autographs, buy your own *shikishi* (a square piece of stiff white paper) before going to the stable. The standard paper for autographs in Japan, *shikishi* can be purchased in the stationery section of any department store for about $1.50. Don't forget to bring a pen. A thick, dark black, permanent marker or *fude* (brush pen) works best on a *shikishi*. Only sekitori wrestlers are allowed to sign, so don't bother asking the lower-ranked ones.

10. When practice is over, guests are usually asked to leave. Unless the wrestlers are willing to stay after, do not harass them for autographs or pictures; otherwise you may have to deal with a less friendly tsukebito (attendant). The Hawaiian wrestlers (Akebono, Konishiki, and Musashimaru) are friendly and are almost always willing to talk to guests briefly and sign autographs.

bolically mark the area as sacred. At this time the sekitori will sometimes make *tegata*, the valuable autographed hand prints so eagerly sought by fans and sponsors. A tsukebito (attendant) will assist by preparing the red ink and white paper (*shikishi*). The sekitori then pats his palm on the pad of ink and stamps it on the *shikishi*, leaving a hand print. Depending on the popularity of the wrestler, he may make dozens or even hundreds of *tegata* at one sitting. After the red ink has dried, the sekitori uses a black brush pen to personally sign his name with *kanji* characters on each one.

Wrestlers then take baths in order of their rank (the highest rank goes first). The Japanese style of bathing is to wash the entire body first outside the tub,

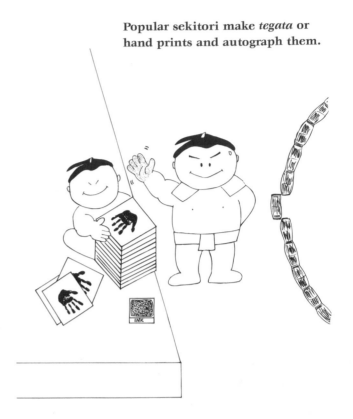

Popular sekitori make *tegata* or hand prints and autograph them.

rinse, and then enter the hot bath only for soaking. When a sekitori wrestler, a coach, or oyakata enters the bathing area, he sits on a small stool and relaxes while a lower-ranked wrestler gives him a massage, scrubs his back with soap, and rinses him off. This custom is quite normal for the Japanese, but many foreign wrestlers have a difficult time adjusting to it.

Sumo wrestlers are notoriously long bath takers. After a hard workout, some soak their aching muscles up to an hour. Attendants must patiently serve them and wait their turn.

Stable Life

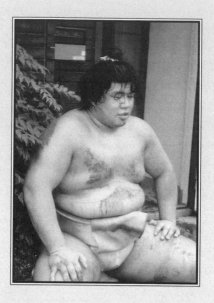

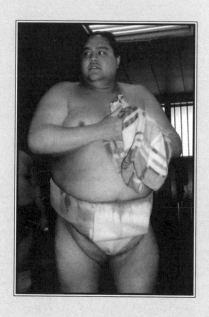

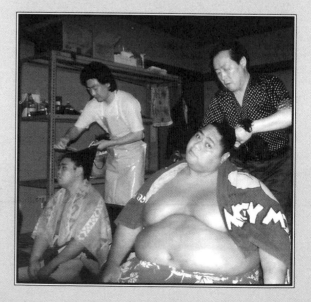

Even after practice, sumo wrestlers are busy. They give interviews, have their hair done, make tegata (hand prints), or go out to social functions. Some young wrestlers have girlfriends, but they are encouraged to wait until they at least reach the juryo level (and are earning a salary) before marrying.

When Jesse Kuhaulua (Azu-mazeki Oyakata, the former Takamiyama) was an active wrestler, it was a struggle for him to do matawari (the splits). One day another wrestler, trying to help him, pushed down on his back, but the pain was so severe that Jesse started to cry. With fierce determination, Jesse protested, "I'm not crying! It's sweat coming out of eyes!" (Namida ja nai! Me kara deta ase yo!).

CHANKONABE: SUMO STEW

Because wrestlers are not allowed to eat breakfast, lunch is the first meal of the day. After a hard practice on an empty stomach, everyone is hungry. But, like everything else in sumo, rank takes precedence. The coaches, oyakata, seki-tori, and invited guests eat while being served by the makushita and lower-ranked wrestlers. The makushita wrestlers are then, in turn, served by the sandanme wrestlers, and so on. Thus, the lowest-ranked wrestlers, who got up earliest, must wait and eat last. It is also lower-ranked wrestlers on "chanko duty" who must do the shopping and cooking, sometimes with the help of the okamisan, the stable-master's wife.

A group of sumo wrestlers eating is quite an amazing scene. Not only do they inhale their food at an incredible pace, but the amount they can consume is astonishing! Eating is a part of the sumo wrestler's job they all take seriously.

A sumotori's meal, whether it be stew, salad, steak, chicken, or rice, is called *chanko*, and the communal meal that is eaten almost every day in the training stable is called *chankonabe*. It is a high-calorie but nutritious stew cooked in a large pot (*nabe*) and served in the stable's dining area. There are several types of *chanko-nabe*. Typical ingredients include:

BASE (usually one or two of the following is used to flavor the stock): *shoyu* (soy sauce), *miso* (soybean paste), *mirin* (sweet sake), chicken bones, garlic, ginger, sesame seed oil, *konbu* (kelp), *katsuo-bushi* (dried bonito)

MEAT (one or two): fish, chicken, pork, beef, weiners, shrimp, clam, squid, crab

OTHER ADDITIONS: *kinoko* (mushrooms), onions, tofu, eggplant, Chinese cabbage, seaweed, eggs, kim-chee, daikon,

Sumo wrestlers chowing down at lunchtime.

konnyaku (a gelatinous substance made from a kind of potato), carrots, radish, spinach, *mochi* (glutinous rice cake), *udon* noodles

Below are a few simple *chankonabe* recipes (all the ingredients can be found in Japanese or Asian grocery stores).

SOPPU DAKKI CHANKONABE

1. Make a soup broth by boiling a chicken bone in water and *shoyu* (soy sauce).

2. Add bite-size pieces of chicken to the broth.

3. Add chopped vegetables—carrots, daikon, *kinoko*, onions, *konnyaku*, cabbage, spinach, etc.

4. Add tofu to the soup.

Udon noodles or *mochi* is sometimes added to the soup as a finale. *Soppu* style is generally used when there are a lot of people to be served.

KIM-CHEE-STYLE CHANKONABE

1. Make a soup broth by boiling sliced pieces of pork in water.

2. Add *miso* and kim-chee base to taste.

3. In a separate pot, boil assorted chopped vegetables—onions, carrots, bean sprouts, etc.

4. Add the boiled vegetables along with *aburage* (deep-fried tofu) to the main pot.

5. Add oysters or some type of seafood.

6. In a separate bowl, beat a couple of raw eggs.

7. When the stew starts to boil, slowly pour the beaten eggs into the stew.

8. Just before serving, add Chinese cabbage and green onions.

MIZUTAKI CHANKONABE

1. Cook fish in a pot of boiling water.

2. Flavor with *shoyu*, sugar, *mirin*, and sake.

3. Add tofu and an assortment of vegetables—Chinese cabbage, carrots, bean sprouts, mushrooms, spinach, green onions, etc.

4. When the vegetables are done, pick the food from the large pot and dip it in a sauce consisting of *shoyu*, vinegar, minced daikon, and green onions.

TSUMIRE-STYLE CHANKONABE

1. Mince sardines, mackerel, and squid and place in a large bowl.

2. Flavor the fish with miso and *mirin*.

3. Add grated *yama imo* (yam).

4. Add minced ginger, garlic, and green onions and mix thoroughly.

5. Shape the mixture into small balls (like bite-size meatballs).

6. Place the balls in a large pot of boiling water.

7. Just before serving, add an assortment of vegetables—spinach, mushrooms, green onions, tofu, etc. Be careful not to overcook the vegetables.

Whatever the type of *chankonabe*, it is always served with large amounts of rice and many other side dishes such as fried fish or chicken, pickled vegetables, *sashimi*, fruits, eggs, salad, and fried rice. The wrestlers eat *chankonabe* every day, but since many different varieties can be made by simply changing the ingredients or spices, no two servings taste exactly alike. During tournaments, chicken is the preferred *chanko* because a chicken stands on two feet (a cow stands on four, which represents defeat in a bout). Wrestlers drink tea, water, beer, or a sports drink with their meals.

AFTER PRACTICE HOURS

After eating lunch and cleaning up the kitchen area, lower-ranked wrestlers start their next round of daily chores. First they must clean the entire stable, sweeping the floors, taking out the trash, cleaning the bathrooms, and straightening up the bedroom areas. The *mawashi* that were worn during practice are laid out to dry. Rikishi then start the laundry. Not only does a lower-ranked wrestler do his own laundry, but he must also do the laundry of his *ani-deshi* (senior) or the sekitori wrestler he is assigned to. Once the daily chores are completed, the sumotori are usually free for the rest of the day. If they stay at the *heya*, they change into comfortable, loose-fitting wear provided by the stable or into their favorite sweatsuits. If they decide to go out to karaoke, to nightclubs, to eat with a sponsor, or even just to run errands, they must wear traditional Japanese garb, either a *yukata* (light cotton dressing gown) or a kimono, depending on their rank. Lower-ranked wrestlers will often accompany a sekitori or a coach to their appointments and carry their belongings or act as bodyguards. If a wrestler has no plans, he usually retreats to the communal room upstairs and takes a nap. (It is said that sleeping is also part of a sumotori's job; taking a nap immediately after eating is the key to gaining the necessary fighting weight.) Around 4:30 pm, those wrestlers assigned to kitchen duty for the day will begin preparations for dinner.

In their free time, many wrestlers love to relax by heading to the local pachinko parlor, playing Nintendo or other video games, reading *manga* (Japanese comics), or going out to sing karaoke.

RANKING

The number of active wrestlers in professional sumo is always changing. Currently there are over eight hundred. A wrestler's lifestyle within his own stable and his treatment by others outside the stable will depend solely upon his rank. Generally, if a wrestler has a winning record, *kachikoshi*, he will go up in rank. If he has a losing record, *makekoshi*, he will go down. In the upper ranks (juryo and makuuchi), a tournament consists of fifteen bouts and a winning record is therefore anything better than 8–7; in the lower divisions, with only seven matches per tournament, a winning record is 4–3.

Wrestlers ranked as ozeki are not demoted unless they suffer two consecutive losing records. Wrestlers who are injured during a tournament and forced to withdraw will have their remaining matches counted as forfeits (losses), but they can apply for an exemption so they can sit out the next tournament and not risk further demotion. Yokozuna are never demoted;

instead, if a yokozuna starts to lose consistently, he is encouraged to retire and save face.

The ranking system in the world of sumo wrestling represents a pyramidal hierarchy with the fewest number of wrestlers at the top (yokozuna) and the majority at the bottom (jonokuchi and jonidan divisions). The lowest rank is *maezumo* ("pre"-sumo). All new recruits start at this qualifying level (except those with outstanding college records, who are allowed to enter from the bottom of the makushita division). Maezumo wrestlers are formally introduced during a tournament in a ceremony called *shusse hiro*, for which occasion they borrow a fancy *kesho mawashi* from a sekitori wrestler in their stable or from their oyakata. *Maezumo* wrestlers compete only against each other in their first tournament. At the next tournament they are ranked at the very bottom of the jonokuchi division, and their names appear on the *banzuke* or ranking sheet for the first time.

Makuuchi Division

Yokozuna

Ozeki

Sekiwake

SANYAKU RANK

Komusubi

Maegashira

Juryo Division

Makushita Division

Sandanme Division

Jonidan Division

Jonokuchi Division

Banzuke-gai (Maezumo)

Sekitori wrestlers

31

JONOKUCHI DIVISION

(Tournament consists of seven matches)
Tournament allowance: $700
Tournament champion: $1,000
No. of wrestlers: varies (100 in 1997)

YUKATA

BAREFOOT
WITH *GETA*

If a wrestler is injured during a tournament he may sit out the next tournament without affecting his ranking. No allowance, however, is made for injuries that occur in practice, during an exhibition, or outside of the ring.

KIMONO

BAREFOOT
WITH *GETA*

JONIDAN DIVISION

(Tournament consists of seven matches)
Tournament allowance: $750
Tournament champion: $2,000
No. of wrestlers: varies (358 in 1997)

*HAORI/
HAKAMA*

BAREFOOT
WITH *SETTA*

SANDANME DIVISION

(Tournament consists of seven matches)

Tournament allowance: $850

Tournament champion: $3,000

No. of wrestlers: 200 (ranked 1–100, East and West)

If a wrestler is in the sandanme division or lower for five years or thirty tournaments (without reaching a higher rank), he must retire.

Some outstanding college wrestlers who were allowed to enter sumo from the bottom of the makushita division include Wajima, Asashio, Mainoumi, Musoyama, Tosanoumi, Tomonohana, Higonoumi, Hamanoshima, Asanowaka, and Dejima.

COAT

TABI
WITH *SETTA*

MAKUSHITA DIVISION

(Tournament consists of seven matches)

Tournament allowance: $1,200

Tournament champion: $5,000

No. of wrestlers: 120 (ranked 1–60, East and West)

JURYO: THE BIG JUMP

There is a saying that the difference between the top of makushita and the bottom of juryo is like *ten to chi*, or "heaven and hell." Even the number-one ranked makushita wrestler is still an apprentice and must serve others. But for the lowest-ranked wrestler in juryo, it's like making the final cut in the major leagues. Only one out of ten wrestlers reaches juryo. He has graduated from the apprentice stage and is now considered a professional wrestler, a sekitori. It is from this level that a wrestler begins to receive a monthly salary and other bonuses and privileges. These include:

wearing a white *mawashi* during practice

wearing a silk *mawashi* and *sagari* (decorative strings) during tournaments

being assigned a couple of tsukebito (attendants) to take care of his personal needs (running errands, doing laundry, serving meals, giving massages, carrying luggage, and even acting as bodyguards)

receiving a *kesho-mawashi* (ceremonial apron)

receiving an *akeni* (bamboo trunk)

participating in the *dohyo-iri* (ring-entering ceremony)

A wrestler who has reached the juryo rank is considered a professional and no longer an apprentice. He is allowed to scold the young wrestlers and use a bamboo stick for instilling discipline.

carrying a fancy Japanese-style umbrella (lower-ranked wrestlers have no choice but to get wet)

being excused from stable chores

getting his own private room

being able to wear a silk kimono

getting his hair styled in the fancy *oichomage*

being allowed to sleep in later

taking a bath and eating first

making *tegata* (hand prints) and signing autographs

having his own personal fan club

being allowed to marry (in most cases, a wrestler must wait until he reaches this level before he receives his oyakata's permission)

WHITE *MAWASHI*

34

JURYO DIVISION

(Tournament consists of fifteen matches)
Tournament champion: $20,000
Monthly salary: $8,700
No. of wrestlers: 26 (ranked 1–13, East and West)

FANCY TOPKNOT
(OICHOMAGE)

FORMAL CRESTED
HAORI/HAKAMA

TABI
WITH *SETTA*

A juryo-level wrestler is entitled to throw salt and use power water for purification.

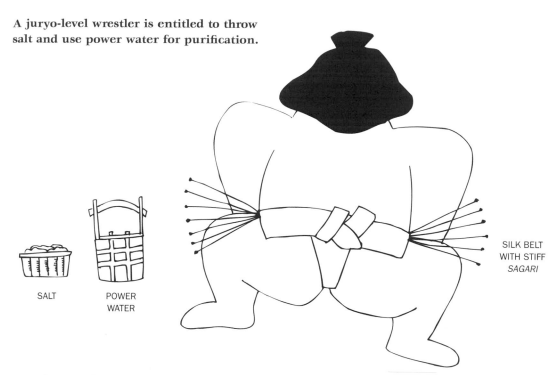

SALT

POWER WATER

SILK BELT WITH STIFF *SAGARI*

Along with the prestige of becoming a sekitori wrestler, however, comes responsibility. A sekitori must always behave in a dignified manner so as not to embarrass his stable or the Sumo Association. Every time he goes somewhere it becomes a big public event, and every word he says is scrutinized by the press. He must become the leader of his stable and assist in the training of young recruits. He should give advice to apprentices and is expected to pick up the tab and treat them when going out. Following Japanese custom, sekitori wrestlers must also give appropriate gifts on ceremonial occasions (such as weddings, parties, or funerals) to coaches, elders, sponsors, and others related to the stable or its affiliates.

A *kesho-mawashi* is a handmade silk apron worn for the *dohyo-iri* (ring-entering ceremony). A sekitori's first one is often given to him by his hometown fan club. Most have gold or silver trim (only ozeki and yokozuna can have purple). The cost for one starts at around $5,000 but can go as high as $20,000! The entire apron and belt are one long, connected piece.

The sekitori is encouraged to donate some of his time to charity and is obligated to make public appearances. For a company president or executive, there is no better way to impress colleagues than to have a high-ranking wrestler at a function. The sekitori generally brings along a couple of his tsukebito. After dinner, he gives a short speech or sings a karaoke song and then signs autographs and poses for pic-

tures. Because there may be hundreds of people at a party, the photo session can be very long. Usually, except for blinking in between the flashes, the sekitori doesn't even move as his fans line up one after another to take a picture. Almost always, at the end of the party, the sekitori is handed an envelope filled with cash. This is called his *kuruma-dai,* or "transportation fare," but in actuality it is a payment for his time. Depending on the event and his popularity, a wrestler can make hundreds or thousands of dollars in one evening. However, a smart sekitori doesn't keep all of the cash to himself. He will usually share the money with his attendants, guaranteeing their devoted and attentive service.

When a wrestler reaches the juryo level, all of the active wrestlers in his entering class (those who joined sumo at the same time) pitch in to buy an *akeni* or trunk to congratulate him on becoming a new sekitori. *Akeni* are used to hold personal belongs and are hand-painted green, with the borders and characters for the wrestler's name in red. *Akeni* are made out of bamboo reinforced with steel rods. They are covered with *washi* (Japanese handmade paper) and then lacquered. The wrestler's tsukebito carries the heavy trunk for him when commuting to tournaments or exhibitions.

MAKUUCHI DIVISION

MAEGASHIRA RANK

Kinboshi (gold star): $250

Monthly salary: $10,990

No. of maegashira: between 28 and 32 (the number depends on the higher ranks; ranked 1–14 to 1–16, East and West)

KOMUSUBI & SEKIWAKE RANK (SANYAKU)

Bonus for those who compete in at least eleven of the fifteen days in a tournament: $500

Monthly salary: $14,210

No. of komusubi: 2–4

No. of sekiwake: 2–4

In the makuuchi division there are five ranks: maegashira, komusubi and sekiwake, ozeki, and yokozuna.

For these upper-ranked wrestlers, a tournament consists of fifteen matches.

The winner of one of the three *sansho* awards gets $20,000 (see pages 80–81).

The winner of the entire tournament gets $100,000.

Each *kensho-kin* ("encouragement money") banner displayed before a bout is worth $300 to the winning wrestler. See page 69.

Promotion to Ozeki

A sekiwake's record over three tournaments is evaluated.

The Sumo Association holds a meeting discussing the candidate. The standard number is thirty-three wins over three tournaments.

A formal acceptance ceremony is held with Sumo Association representatives, the wrestler, and his oyakata and the oyakata's wife. The new ozeki receives a one-time bonus called *meiyokin* (honor money) of $5,000.

OZEKI RANK

Bonus for those who compete in at least eleven of the fifteen days in a tournament: $1,500

Monthly salary: $19,710

No. of ozeki: varies; generally 2–4

Congratulations! You've been promoted!

Recent Ozeki Promotion Records

WRESTLER	2 TOURN. BEFORE	1 TOURN. BEFORE	DECIDING TOURN.	3 TOURN. TOTAL
Konishiki	10–5	11–4	12–3	33–12
Asahifuji	10–5	11–4	12–3	33–12
Kirishima	10–5	11–4	13–2	34–11
Akebono	13–2	8–7	13–2*	34–11
Takanohana	14–1*	10–5	11–4	35–10
Wakanohana	14–1*	10–5	13–2	37–8
Musashimaru	8–7	13–2	12–3	33–12
Takanonami	10–5	12–3	13–2	35–10

* = tournament champion

If the promotion is approved, a messenger is sent to the stable to deliver the news.

Only about 1 in 400 rikishi makes ozeki rank.

Promotion to Yokozuna

An ozeki who wins two tournaments in a row (or has an equivalent record) is evaluated.

The Yokozuna Council (up to fifteen members) holds a meeting. Promotion must be by unanimous decision.

A candidate must have dignity (hinkaku) and be exceptionally strong in the dohyo.

Head of Sumo Association.

Omedetogozaimasu! Congratulations!

Recent Yokozuna Promotion Records

WRESTLER	1 TOURN. BEFORE	DECIDING TOURN.	2 TOURN. TOTAL
Chiyonofuji	13–2	14–1*	27–3
Takanosato	13–2	14–1*	27–3
Futahaguro	12–3	14–1	26–4
Hokutoumi	12–3*	13–2	25–5
Onokuni	12–3	13–2	25–5
Asahifuji	14–1*	14–1*	28–2
Akebono	14–1*	13–2*	27–3
Takanohana	15–0*	15–0*	30–0

* = tournament champion

If the promotion is approved, a messenger is sent to the stable to deliver the news. A formal acceptance ceremony is held with Sumo Association representatives, the wrestler, and his oyakata and the oyakata's wife.

YOKOZUNA RANK

Bonus for those who compete in at least eleven of the fifteen days in a tournament: $2,000

Monthly salary: $23,690

No. of yokozuna: varies; generally 1–3

The new yokozuna receives a one-time bonus called *meiyokin* (honor money) of $10,000.

Only about 1 in 800 rikishi makes yokozuna rank.

Yokozuna Formal Acceptance Ceremony

SHIRANUI STYLE

UNRYU STYLE

The new yokozuna and his oyakata must decide on the style of the *yokozuna dohyo-iri* and the special belt, the *yokozuna tsuna*.

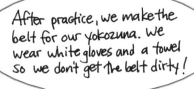

After practice, we make the belt for our yokozuna. We wear white gloves and a towel so we don't get the belt dirty!

The yokozuna's ceremonial belt weighs anywhere from 30 to 40 pounds and is about 13 feet long; each is custom made to fit the wrestler. The belt is white and must be kept as clean as possible. The yokozuna's tsukebito use brushes to keep dust and sand off the belt, and white powder to cover minor scuffs. The cost of the belt depends on its size, but it is usually around several thousand dollars. Each yokozuna is given an allowance from the Sumo Association to help cover the cost. The belt is then assembled by the yokozuna's stablemates.

Towel

The new yokozuna is formally installed at Tokyo's Meiji Shrine before thousands of well-wishers and fans. Here the wrestler performs his first yokozuna *dohyo-iri,* the special ring-entering ceremony that involves calling the gods and chasing away demons by clapping the hands and stamping the feet. The ceremony is also performed each day of a tournament. See pages 58–61 for more information.

Tsunauchi-shiki:
The Yokozuna Belt-making Ceremony

A yokozuna has a new white tsuna or belt made for him after his initial promotion and before every tournament held in Tokyo thereafter (there are three Tokyo tournaments each year). To prepare the belt, the yokozuna's stablemates soften hemp cloth by rubbing it with powder. Once the hemp cloth is soft, it is put aside to be used later as stuffing or padding. The outside of the belt is made from three strips of a special cotton and silk fabric. The strips are tied to the teppo pole in the corner of the practice area and are twisted and woven. The padding is inserted, and copper wires are then placed inside the belt to stiffen it. Any extra material is cut off, and the small left-over pieces are given away to sponsors or friends of the yokozuna as good luck charms.

During the belt-making ceremony, a stable will often call an affiliate stable to come over and participate. It takes around fifteen men to twist and weave the belt into shape. One wrestler is usually assigned to beat a Japanese-style drum to keep the rhythm as the wrestlers weave in unison. Each belt is custom fit and measured. When the belt is finished, it takes several wrestlers to tie it on the yokozuna.

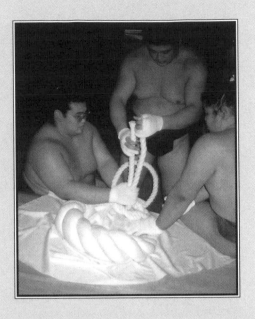

BANZUKE: THE RANKING SHEET

The sumo rankings are posted thirteen days before every tournament on a sheet called a *banzuke*. (The ranking sheet for the January tournament is released before New Year's Day, about sixteen days before the tournament.) Working on a large piece of paper, a high-ranking sumo gyoji, or referee, carefully writes down the *kanji* characters of all the ranked wrestlers in a fancy calligraphy called *sumo-moji* (sumo lettering). The *banzuke* takes about a week to complete. With so many names to write and such little space to work with, the gyoji must be very skilled to make the *banzuke* look artful and balanced. The work is tightly guarded before the official rankings announcement. The *banzuke* is then printed at reduced size on sheets measuring 15 x 21 inches, and copies are distributed by the Sumo Association. The stables buy a large quantity of the ranking sheets and send them out to their sponsors. The *chaya,* or tea houses in the Kokugikan, also buy a supply to give to their patrons. Fans can purchase *banzuke* at the tournament site for a small fee.

On the *banzuke*, the wrestlers are divided into East (on the right) and West (on the left). The East is the more prestigious side. Along with the wrestlers' names are their hometown and rank. The names at the top represent the makuuchi wrestlers. Below the makuuchi are the lower divisions. The size of the print gets smaller with the rankings, until at the very bottom it becomes quite difficult to read. Included on the *banzuke* are the names of the referees, ring attendants, judges, and elders.

A print of sumo's top makuuchi division. The Hawaiian wrestlers are portrayed along the top right row. The official banzuke *(with an inset detailing the special sumo lettering) is shown at right.*

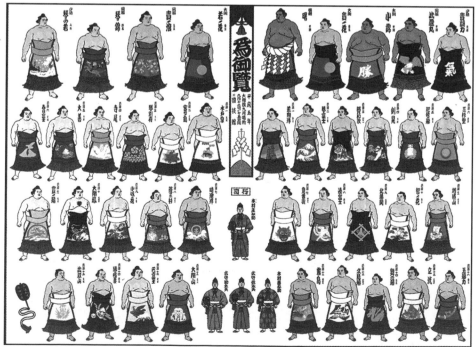

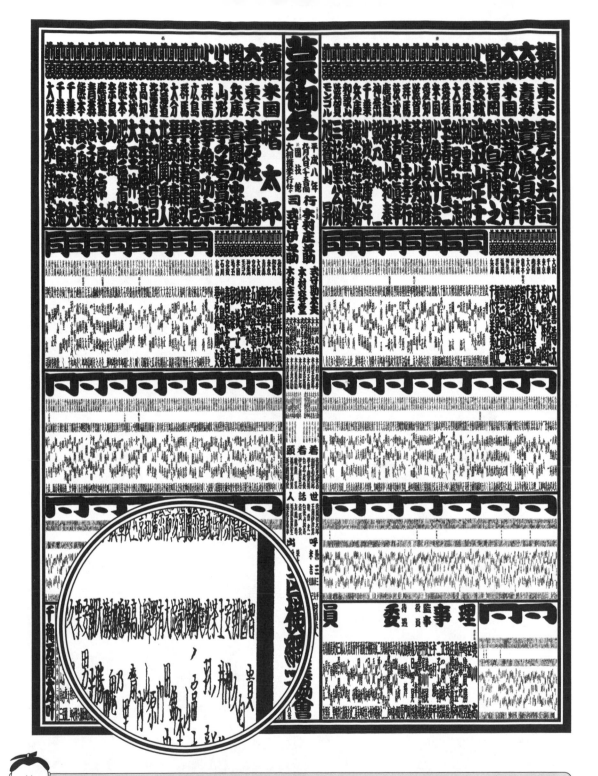

Although the rankings are carefully guarded before the official announcement, promotions to yokozuna, first-time ozeki, and juryo are made known in advance in order to give the promoted wrestlers time to prepare for their new responsibilities. Yokozuna and ozeki must take part in special ceremonies. First-time juryo wrestlers need time to have their first *kesho-mawashi* and kimono made. The easiest way to obtain an official *banzuke* is to go to the Kokugikan in Ryogoku the day after it is published (the Tuesday thirteen days before a tournament). The Sumo Association sells a limited number of them at a desk near the main entrance. Go early because they sell out quickly.

Life in the Ranks of Sumo

Japan is a very hierarchical society. A person's speech and mannerisms are all determined by rank or status, and by the rank or status of the person he is talking to. Sumo, the most traditional Japanese sport, is no exception. Every person in the entire Sumo Association knows where he stands and must act accordingly. Within the stable itself, lower-ranked wrestlers must serve the upper-ranked, and eat and bathe only after others are done.

Regardless of rank, sumo wrestlers are dignified warriors and must always be humble (note: the wrestler bowing). But a sumo wrestler's life is an uphill battle. If he can become a sekitori he receives many privileges, such as being able to participate in the dohyo-iri, getting permission to marry, and having his own personal cushions and akeni (lacquered boxes). The akeni is transported for tournaments and exhibitions by the wrestler's tsukebito. Inside the akeni are the wrestler's mawashi (belt), kesho-mawashi (ceremonial apron), and other personal belongings.

HONBASHO: TOURNAMENTS

There are six *honbasho* or major tournaments a year. They are held every other month. All of the tournaments, except for the Nagoya Basho, begin on the second Sunday of the month and end two weeks later, on the fourth Sunday. The Nagoya Basho begins on the first Sunday in July. In between the tournaments are several *jungyo* (exhibitions) held all over Japan and occasionally abroad, but their outcomes have no bearing on the rankings.

NHK (the government-owned radio and TV broadcaster that has carried sumo since 1953) and Radio Kanto broadcast the tournaments live every day from about 3 pm to 6 pm. At 11 pm Asahi TV hosts "Sumo Digest," a thirty-minute program showing the makuuchi matches (and cutting out all the rituals before each bout).

The Tokyo tournaments are held in the Ryogoku district of Sumida Ward (northeastern Tokyo) at the Kokugikan, a $150-million stadium that opened in 1985 and can hold up to 13,000 spectators (in seats and standing-room areas). Because of the limited number of tournaments, tickets to watch sumo live can be extremely difficult to obtain. Even the wrestlers themselves have a tough time getting tickets for their own family members.

The Kokugikan arena at Ryogoku. It also houses the Sumo Association offices, a museum, a sumo training school, and souvenir and snack shops.

SUNAKABURI SEATS

Tickets go on sale about one month before the start of each tournament. The best seats in the stadium are the first six rows, called *sunakaburi*, the "sand-covered" seats (because spectators there sometimes find themselves covered with sand from the ring, or a toppling wrestler). These seats are so close to the *dohyo* that, although it is not recommended, you can actually touch a seated wrestler waiting to go on. There are no barriers or guards separating the wrestlers and judges from the spectators. Unfortunately, these close-up seats are usually not offered to the public but are given to the Sumo Association's patrons. They are also the only seats where eating or drinking is not permitted.

MASU-ZEKI SEATS

Next up from the *sunakaburi* are the Japanese-style tatami boxes with cushions, *masu-zeki*, that seat four people. These seats can be purchased from the *chaya* (tea houses that are in the north entrance of the stadium) or through the Ticket Pia agency. They are expensive and very difficult to obtain without good connections;

In the United States you can watch sumo live via satellite dish. The settings are: Satellite Galaxy 6 (over the equator at 74° west), transponder 6, vertical polarity, C-band NTSC. For audio, 6.2 is Japanese, and 6.8 is English. Broadcasts are from 2:30 am EST for about ninety minutes. Using the smaller digital satellite through Primestar you can get NHK's coverage on the pay channel TV/Japan. For information call Primestar at 1-800-PRIMESTAR or TV Japan at 1-800-518-8576.

THE TOURNAMENT CALENDAR

MONTH	TOURNAMENT NAME	LOCATION
January	Hatsu (First) Basho	Tokyo: Kokugikan
March	Haru (Spring) Basho	Osaka: Osaka Prefectural Gymnasium
May	Natsu (Summer) Basho	Tokyo: Kokugikan
July	Nagoya Basho	Nagoya: Aichi Prefectural Gymnasium
September	Aki (Fall) Basho	Tokyo: Kokugikan
November	Kyushu Basho	Fukuoka: Fukuoka International Center

large corporations generally buy them up, much like the best seats at American football games. When you purchase a ticket for the *masu-zeki*, you not only pay for the seat, but for food, drinks, and programs that are brought out to you by an usher. The menu usually consists of *yakitori*, *musubi*, *mochi*, Japanese pastries, beer, and so on. With the food, drinks, and four people, space in a single *masu-zeki* is very limited. If you are fortunate enough to sit in a *masu-zeki*, be sure to wear comfortable clothes; there are no chairs, and you will have to take your shoes off before you set foot on the tatami.

> Price: A tickets $111 (per person)
> B tickets $101
> C tickets $91

You must buy an entire box (seats four). For reservations, contact a *chaya* at the Kokugikan (03-3263-5111), Ticket Pia (03-5237-9999), or your hotel concierge.

SECOND-FLOOR SEATS

Up on the second floor are regular Western-style seats with arm rests and cup holders. Although the seats are far from the *dohyo*, the view is quite good, and watching the action live, even if from the second floor, is still much more exciting than on television.

> Price: A tickets $81
> B tickets $61
> C tickets $36

For reservations in Tokyo contact Ticket Pia about three weeks before a tournament. Most of the good seats sell out on the first day, but if you are among the lucky ones to get through and make a reservation, you must pick up your tickets within one week at any Ticket Pia outlet. Or you can have them mailed to you and pay by registered mail or by bank transfer.

TOJITSU-KEN

During tournaments, there are a limited number of daily tickets (about 500) called *tojitsu-ken*. These tickets are for the upper rows on the second floor and are relatively inexpensive, but they cannot be bought in advance. They can only be purchased (one per person) at the Kokugikan in the morning, and they must be used that same day.

> Price: $21

Chaya, *or tea houses, within the Kokugikan.*

Masuzeki (box seats) are small and crowded, but the price includes food service.

The box office opens at 9 am, with lines for these tickets usually starting to form around 7 am or earlier. Weekend tickets, especially on the last Sunday, sell out very quickly, so you will probably have a better chance of getting a ticket on a weekday.

If after all of this you still come up empty handed, the last resort is to buy tickets from the scalpers, called *dafuya*, outside of the Kokugikan. You cannot miss them—they are usually *yakuza* (gangsters) with the requisite sunglasses, lit cigarettes, and cellular phones. They wait outside of the entrance waving tickets and yelling *"Kippu ga nai hito!"* (Anyone who doesn't have a ticket!). Although prices can be negotiated a little, the scalper's service fee makes the tickets more expensive than their face value. When buying more than one ticket, check to make sure that the seats are together. Scalpers will only accept cash, in Japanese yen. Depending on the seat, weekday tickets sell for $70–$100, and weekend tickets for $100–$500. Be careful, however, since buying tickets from scalpers, as in the U.S., is technically against the law.

Inside, the simplicity and beauty of the sumo arena is breathtaking. The *dohyo* in the center of the

Each decorative tassel or fusa *above the* dohyo *represents one of the four seasons: green = spring, red = summer, white = autumn, black = winter.*

ground floor is hand built with picks and shovels before every Tokyo tournament by about twenty yobidashi (ring attendants) working over a period of three days. About 30 tons of clay (8 if only the top is resurfaced) are brought in and pounded down to form the ring and surrounding square-shaped platform. *Tawara*, or bales of rice straw, are half-buried in the clay to create the circular boundary of the fighting area. In all, some 66 *tawara* are used in the construction of the *dohyo*:

20   the ring, including the 4 *tokudawara*; *tokudawara* are the bales that are a few inches outside of the circle; their original purpose was to help drain rain from the ring area during bouts in olden times when sumo was held outdoors

4   holders for power water

4   the corners

10   the steps

28   the squared-off area outside of the ring

Each *tawara* is made by hand and filled with clay, sand, or a rock-and-sand combination. Finally, the two *shikiri-sen*, or starting lines where the initial clash takes place, are painted just over 2 feet apart on the east and west sides in the center of the ring. When a sumo tournament is not being held in the Kokugikan, the entire ring can be lowered to an underground storage area, allowing the arena to be used for other events.

Following completion of the *dohyo*, on the day before the tournament begins a Shinto ceremony known as the *dohyo matsuri* is held. A high-level gyoji (referee) performs the rite, offering sacred foods and sake and praying for the safety of the rikishi during the battles to come.

Directly above the *dohyo*

Tournament Etiquette

A spectator should never pass between a judge and the *dohyo*.

The *dohyo* is considered sacred; spectators should never touch it, even after the matches are completed.

Taking photographs is permitted, but spectators must remain in their seats. Only official press photographers are allowed to take photographs near the *dohyo* and from the aisles.

Spectators should not throw their *zabuton* (seating cushions) into the *dohyo* (although sometimes after a big upset, this inevitably happens).

hangs a 6-ton *tsuriyane*, or Shinto-style roof. At one time the roof was supported by pillars, but their massive size blocked the view of too many spectators. In 1952 the pillars were removed, and the roof was suspended from the ceiling. In each corner of the roof is a *fusa*, or tassel. A purple curtain called the *mizuhiki-maku*, emblazoned with the Sumo Association crest, hangs down from the *tsuriyane*.

Above the second-floor seats on all four sides of the arena are larger-than-life-size portraits of past tournament champions. Since color photographs fade over time, a black-and-white photo taken of the champion wrestler in a studio is blown up to about 10 feet in height and then colorized by an artist. The entire process takes about one week. After the finished picture is framed, the champion's name and rank and the date of the tournament are written in fancy *kanji* characters. Viewing the portraits of winning wrestlers is like instantly taking in a little bit of sumo history.

The four aisles that lead to the *dohyo* are called the *hanamichi*, or flower paths. The two aisles on the southeast and southwest sides are for wrestlers to use as they walk from the dressing rooms to the ring.

The draw, or *torikumi*, is made the day before each day's bouts (except for the first two days' bouts it is made two days in advance). Wrestlers are generally matched against those closest in rank, although lower-ranked wrestlers with good tournament records may be pitted against higher-ranking opponents. Yokozuna usually tackle the komusubi wrestlers first and then the ozeki during the second week.

Yokozuna fight each other at the end of the tournament. Lower-division wrestlers fight a total of seven matches per tournament; juryo and makuuchi fight fifteen.

The lowest-ranked wrestlers in the jonokuchi division start their matches around 9 am. (On the last day of the tournament, matches usually begin around 10:30 am, since by this day most of the lower divisions have finished their bouts.) Except for a few short breaks when the ringside judges are changed, the matches are continuous until just before 3 pm, when the juryo *dohyo-iri*, or ring-entering ceremony, takes place.

Here is the approximate daily schedule for a typical *basho*:

9:00	Jonokuchi Division
10:00	Jonidan Division
12:00	Sandanme Division
1:30	Makushita Division
2:40	Juryo Division *dohyo-iri* (ring-entering ceremony)
2:50	Juryo Division
3:40	Makuuchi Division *dohyo-iri*
4:00	Makuuchi Division
5:50	Musubi Ichiban (the last match of the day, usually involving the highest-ranked yokozuna); on the final day of the tournament the bouts finish at about 5:30 to allow time for the awards ceremony that follows
6:00	*Yumitori-shiki* (Bow-twirling Ceremony)

Tournament Pageantry

The flags that fly outside the Kokugikan during tournaments are very colorful, but they never use the color black—black represents a kuroboshi or loss. Inside the tsuriyane or roof are microphones and dozens of lightbulbs that help illuminate the dohyo. From the first match until just before the juryo dohyo-iri, only about a third of them are used. Just before the juryo dohyo-iri starts, all of them are turned on. Above the tsuriyane hang banners with the characters man-in onrei ("full house, thank you"). At the bottom of this page is a close-up view of a tawara. On the facing page is the denkoban or scoreboard; the kanji characters of each rikishi's name are written by a gyoji on thin rectangular sheets of plastic.

A larger-than-life-size portrait of each champion wrestler is hung at the Kokugikan arena. There is only enough space on the Kokugikan walls for the champions of the past five and a half years. The wrestler is also given a small framed copy of the portrait for his own collection. On the first day of each Tokyo basho, the new portraits of the last two tournament champions are revealed. From top left, clockwise: Konishiki, Kitano-umi, Akebono, Takanohana.

JURYO AND MAKUUCHI DOHYO-IRI

Before the juryo and makuuchi matches, the traditional *dohyo-iri* or ring-entering ceremony takes place. All the higher-ranked wrestlers make their appearance wearing the traditional *kesho-mawashi,* a fancy ceremonial apron that hangs down in front to just above the ankle.

The *dohyo-iri* for the juryo and makuuchi divisions is basically the same. Performed before each division's bouts, the ceremony dates back to the Genroku era (1688–1704) when rikishi began wearing *kesho-mawashi* to show off the name of their sponsoring lord. A referee and all the wrestlers in the division make their way down the *hanamichi* aisles to the *dohyo.* The referee enters first, followed by the wrestlers in reverse order of rank. When a wrestler passes a judge on his way to the *dohyo,* he usually bows his head slightly and raises his arm, showing the back of his hand, as a pardon for passing in front of an elder. A rikishi's name, hometown, and stable are announced as he circles the *dohyo.* Just before the first wrestler makes a complete circle around the ring, he stops. After the highest-ranked wrestler (usually an ozeki for the makuuchi division) enters, all of the wrestlers turn inward and in synchronization perform a brief sequence of ritual movements. On odd-numbered days, the East side performs first. On even-numbered days, the West side goes first.

The ring-entering ceremony is exactly the same every day of the tournament, unless a member of the imperial family is present, at which time a special *dohyo-iri* is performed. (In that *dohyo-iri,* wrestlers line up in five lines instead of a circle, all facing the imperial box so that no one's back is toward the royal family.) A yokozuna does not participate in either ceremony. He has his own separate *dohyo-iri,* following that of the makuuchi division.

After the juryo division's *dohyo-iri,*

3.

Raise right arm.

2.

Clap.

1.

Both arms down.

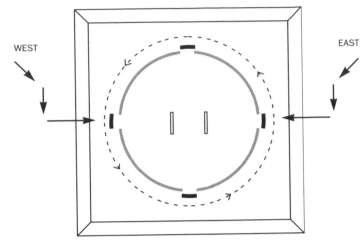

WEST

EAST

Wrestlers enter the *dohyo* from their respective sides and then circle the ring counterclockwise before performing their ritual movements.

4.

Pull up *mawashi* with both hands.

salt, *chikara mizu* (power water), and *chikara gami* (power paper) are placed in the southeast and southwest corners of the *dohyo* for the wrestlers to use during their purification rituals prior to each bout. When the maku-uchi division's *dohyo-iri* is over, the yokozuna, along with his two attendants and the tate-gyoji (head referee), performs his *dohyo-iri* (see page 58).

5.

Raise both arms.

6.

Both arms down.

Significance of the Dohyo-iri

The *dohyo-iri* is a chance for the audience to see all the wrestlers who will fight that day and for the rikishi to show off their impressive *kesho-mawashi*. The synchronized hand and leg motions also have traditional meanings that can be traced to sumo's own Shinto roots. The clapping is to alert the gods and for purification. The raising of the arms is to show that the wrestlers carry no weapons and will play fair. The raising of the *kesho-mawashi*, like the frequent leg-stomping in other sumo rituals, is to drive out evil spirits.

YOKOZUNA DOHYO-IRI

The *yokozuna dohyo-iri* was first performed in 1789 by Tanikaze Kajinosuke. After the makuuchi *dohyo-iri* is complete and the wrestlers have left the *dohyo,* the yokozuna enters the ring with the tate-gyoji (head referee) and two attendants. One attendant is the *tsuyu-harai* (dew sweeper); the other is the higher-ranked *tachimochi* (sword bearer). In ancient times, the sword was a symbol of the yokozuna's samurai status. Both attendants are active wrestlers who must be below ozeki rank but in the makuuchi division. Generally, they are also members or affiliates of the same stable as the yokozuna. If the regular attendant is scheduled to fight either the yokozuna or the other attendant that day, another wrestler will serve in his place.

The yokozuna's *dohyo-iri* starts with a thunderous clap called *chiri o kiru.* This is done for purification and to alert the gods. By extending his arm, the yokozuna shows that he carries no weapons. By stomping his feet in the large sweeping motions called *shiko* he scares away any evil spirits. If there is more than one yokozuna, they will take turns going first, but each yokozuna must perform the ceremony every day of the tournament.

4.

Raise both arms.

1.

At side of ring: clap.

2.

Stretch out arms.

3.

Stand; move to center of ring.

5.

Clap.

The yokozuna *dohyo-iri* looks very simple, but it takes a lot of concentration to perform. As Akebono explained, "You have to focus yourself and put all of your power into it. It is very intense!"

6.

Raise both arms.

7.

Clap.

8.

Right arm outstretched.

9.

Left arm outstretched.

10.

Shiko with right leg.

The length of time it takes to complete the *dohyo-iri* depends on the yokozuna. Each wrestler has his own style and rhythm. Some complete the ritual in less than a minute, while others take three minutes or more.

59

11A.

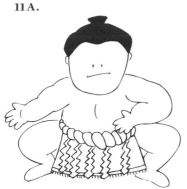

Unryu style: crouch with right arm outstretched.

11B.

Shiranui style: crouch with both arms outstretched.

The *unryu* style of *dohyo-iri* is considered defensive because one hand is held by the chest as a sign of protection. The *shiranui* style adopts a more offensive posture, since the wrestler performs the ceremony with his arms outstretched.

12A.

Unryu style: rise with right arm outstretched.

12B.

Shiranui style: rise with both arms outstretched.

13.

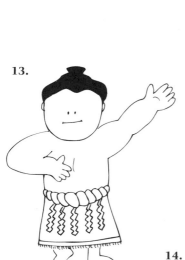

Left arm outstretched.

14.

Shiko with right leg.

15.

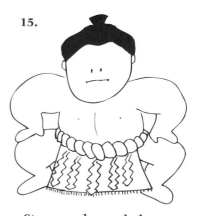

Stomp and crouch down.

Yokozuna Takanohana performing the dohyo-iri.

19.

Rise and stand.

18.

Stomp and crouch down.

17.

Shiko **with left leg.**

16.

Rise and stand, then right arm outstretched.

A yokozuna performs his last *dohyo-iri* on the day of his retirement ceremony. If he lives to be sixty, he performs a ceremonial *kanreki dohyo-iri* (wearing a red *tsuna*). Reaching your sixtieth birthday is an important occasion in Japan and is celebrated by wearing something red.

Entering the Ring

The colorful pageantry of the dohyo-iri. This page, clockwise from top left: wrestlers performing rituals; filing in; a close-up shot of Tochinowaka, Kyokudozan, and Wakashoyo; yokozuna Akebono raises his arms high; yokozuna Takanohana proudly poses.

This page, clockwise from top left: yokozuna Takanohana displaying his picture-perfect shiko and then posing with his arm outstretched; a backside view of makuuchi wrestler Asahiyutaka; a close-up of the yokozuna tsuna or belt; Takanohana flanked by his attendants, Takatoriki and Naminohama.

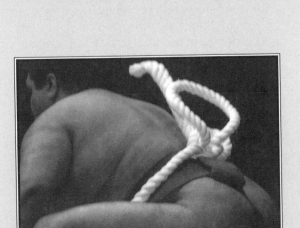

SHIKIRI: PRE-BOUT RITUALS

After the *dohyo-iri*, wrestlers return to the *shitakubeya*, or locker room, where they take off their *kesho-mawashi* and put on regular *mawashi*. They wait for their bouts in the locker room, where there are no chairs, only elevated tatami mats. Two TVs hanging down from the ceiling enable the wrestlers to monitor the bouts. When it is almost his turn, a wrestler will start to make his way down the *hanamichi*. Two bouts before his match he takes a seat at ringside. If he is a makuuchi division wrestler he is allowed to have his own ringside cushion, which a tsukebito brings out for him. When it is time, a yobidashi (ring attendant), holding a fan and using a specially trained high-pitched voice, sings out the names of the two wrestlers who will fight next. After he exits the *dohyo*, the wrestlers step up, bow to each other, and head directly to their corners. Then the gyoji again announces the names of the wrestlers, who at this point have already begun their pre-bout rituals.

In their corners the wrestlers clap

In early sumo there were no time limits on the pre-bout rituals. Wrestlers would begin fighting whenever they were both mentally prepared and ready to go. Sometimes this could take up to 30 minutes for a single bout. It wasn't until 1928, when radio broadcasting of sumo matches began, that time limits were established.

Like the *dohyo-iri*, the pre-bout rituals in sumo have traditional symbolic meanings derived from Shinto beliefs. The time allowed for these rituals is different for each division. In most cases, it actually takes longer to perform the ritual than the bout itself:

DIVISION	TIME
Jonokuchi to Makushita	2 minutes
Juryo	3 minutes
Makuuchi	4 minutes

AT THE WRESTLER'S CORNER

1.

Clap.

their hands and do two *shiko* (leg stomps, first with the right and then with the left leg) to drive out evil spirits as well as limber their legs.

If the match is juryo level or above, the sekitori will then receive *chikara mizu* (power water). The water is for purification and is not swallowed but is used to rinse the mouth and then spit out. Only the wrestler who has won the previous match can give water to the next fighter. Consequently, on one side, a winning wrestler gives the water, and on the other, a fighter from the match to follow gives it (since he has not fought yet, he hasn't lost yet and therefore cannot be unlucky). After rinsing his mouth, the wrestler wipes his mouth, and sometimes body, with *chikara gami* (power paper).

Because the matches are believed to be fought in the presence of the gods, a wrestler's body and mind must be pure. Each time he enters the circular fighting area of the ring, he throws a handful of salt. According to Shinto beliefs, salt drives out evil spirits and has cleansing power.

64

2.

Two *shiko* stomps (first with the right and then with the left leg).

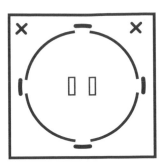

3.

Rinse with *chikara mizu* (power water).

4.

Throw salt and enter ring.

The Shitakubeya

The shitakubeya *is the locker room where wrestlers wait prior to their match. There they limber up, get their hair done, get dressed, or even relax by playing cards.*

AT THE WRESTLER'S SIDE OF THE RING

The fighters go to the east and west sides of the ring and, in unison, squat down on their toes, clap, and extend their arms out horizontally. This is called the *chiri-chozu* ceremony. As before, the clapping is done for purification and to alert the gods that a match is about to take place. The wrestlers then extend their arms to show that they carry no weapons and will play fair.

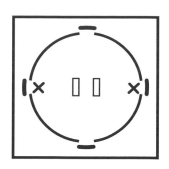

In one day over 88 pounds of salt are tossed out onto the *dohyo* by the wrestlers. (That's over 1,320 pounds a tournament!) There are many different ways sumo wrestlers throw salt. Some throw underhand, some throw side-armed. Some gently lay it in the air, while others slam it into the ground. Some throw handfuls while others toss only a pinch. However, almost all wrestlers throw with their right hand. Take a close look at your favorite wrestler's salt-throwing techniques!

5.

Both arms down.

Before the Match

Wrestlers line up as they wait their turn to go down the hanamichi. A yobidashi, in a beautifully trained voice, calls out the names of those who will wrestle in the next bout.

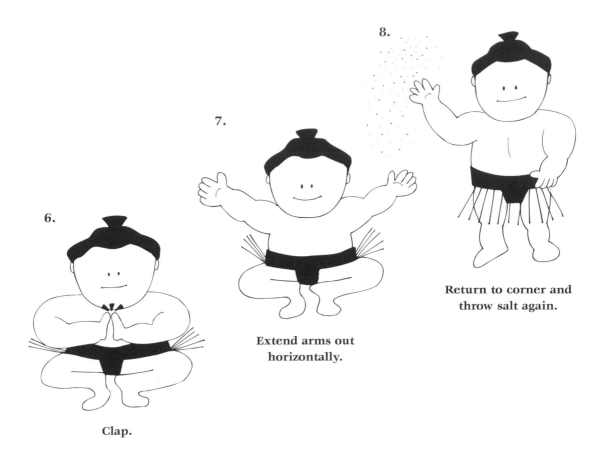

6.

Clap.

7.

Extend arms out
horizontally.

8.

Return to corner and
throw salt again.

AT THE SHIKIRI-SEN
(CENTER STARTING LINES)

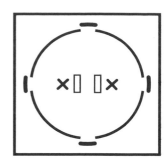

9.

Clap.

10.

Two *shiko* stomps (one with each leg).

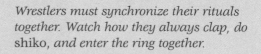

Wrestlers must synchronize their rituals together. Watch how they always clap, do shiko, *and enter the ring together.*

NIRAMIAI

The wrestlers approach the center of the ring. There, in a crouched position, knuckles on the ground, wrestlers stare each other down in a psychological contest known as *niramiai*. This mental battle prior to the bout can be very intense. The wrestlers rise up, return to their corners, toss a handful of salt, and then return to the starting lines, all the while glaring at each other. They do this three or four times. Often, you can predict the winner of the match just by his facial expressions and look of confidence.

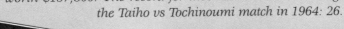

As the wrestlers are performing their pre-bout rituals, parading around the ring can be seen yobi-dashi holding 2-x-4-foot banners representing kensho-kin, *"encouragement money" pledged by companies or sponsors to the winning wrestler of a bout.* Kensho-kin *can be very profitable for a strong sekitori. Each banner represents $600. The winning wrestler receives all the envelopes pledged per bout, but each envelope contains only $300. The Sumo Association takes $50 to cover the cost of making the banner, and another $250 is held in reserve and given to the wrestler at the end of the year to help with his taxes. In 1995, yokozuna Takanohana won 525 flags, worth $157,500! The record for most* kenshokin *in a single bout goes to the Taiho vs Tochinoumi match in 1964: 26.*

Niramiai:
Head to Head

To some Westerners, the rituals and repeated niramiai may seem boring or redundant, but many matches are mentally won during this staredown. The anticipation gradually builds as the wrestlers prepare to battle. Occasionally wrestlers get so psyched that they decide to start before time has expired. Since the wrestlers cannot speak to each other, the decision to charge early is made through eye contact alone.

THE FIGHT

During the warm-up period, the gyoji (referee) guides the wrestlers with commands. If the wrestlers both deem themselves ready to go, they can start their bout early (*jikan mae*). Both must move at the same time. When the allotted time for warm-up and *niramiai* has expired (*jikan ippai*), the gyoji will stand facing forward, call out *"Matta nashi"* or *"Seigen jikan ippai"* ("It's time"), and hold his *gunbai* (war paddle, the referee's symbol of authority) out vertically. Once the gyoji has called time, a wrestler may not leave the center of the ring to fetch salt or water again. If at any point he steps outside the *dohyo*, he forfeits the bout. The tension reaches its climax when the two wrestlers match their breathing and rhythm and without speaking, using only eye contact, touch the ground with both fists and charge at each other. Their initial clash, called *tachi-ai,* must be synchronized. If one wrestler jumps too early, or is not ready (*matta*), the referee will stop the fight and the wrestlers must try again. Juryo wrestlers are fined $500 and makuuchi wrestlers $1,000 for committing *matta*. Either or both wrestlers may be penalized.

Most matches in sumo are very short, concluding within a few seconds. A long bout is one that goes over a minute. Once the fighting starts, the rules are very simple. The loser of a bout is the one who first:

1. steps or falls out of the ring

2. touches the ground with anything but the soles of his feet

3. uses an illegal technique or *kinjite* (e.g., choking, punching, pulling hair, poking the eyes, clapping both ears at once, grabbing in the groin area, or kicking above the knees)

4. has his *mawashi* come completely off (this almost never happens, because the referee, with no penalty to the wrestler, will usually call a time-out—*gyoji matta*—and tighten a wrestler's dangerously loose belt before it falls off)

Officially, there are seventy *kimarite*, or winning techniques, but only about forty-eight are commonly seen. Many are thrusting or pushing techniques, arm throws, or leg trips. Pictured here are a few of the more common techniques (in the illustrations, the winning wrestler is in the black *mawashi*).

YORIKIRI (force out). A wrestler uses both hands on his opponent's belt to force him out.

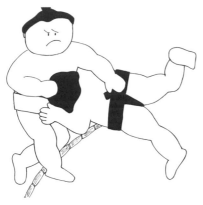

YORITAOSHI (force out and down). Similar to *yorikiri*, except as the wrestler drives out his opponent he topples on him due to either momentum or force.

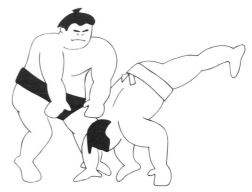

HATAKIKOMI (pull down). A wrestler grabs his opponent's hands, arms, shoulders, or neck and pulls him down.

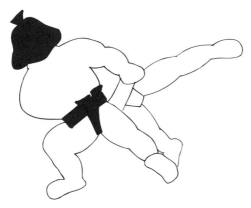

UWATENAGE (overarm throw). The most common throw technique. A wrestler, using an outside grip on the belt, throws his opponent down.

SHITATENAGE (underarm throw). Similar to *uwatenage*, except the wrestler uses an inside grip on the belt to throw his opponent down.

UWATEDASHINAGE (overarm throw-out). A variation of *uwatenage*, except the wrestler throws his opponent out, usually by an outside grip on the back of the belt.

SHITATEDASHINAGE (underarm throw-out). A variation of *shitatenage*, except the wrestler throws his opponent out, usually by an inside grip on the back of the belt.

SUKUINAGE (beltless arm throw). A wrestler forces his arm under his opponent's armpit and then, without gripping the belt, throws him down.

KUBINAGE (headlock throw). A wrestler wraps his arm around his opponent's neck, as in a headlock, and throws his opponent down.

TSURIDASHI (carry out). A wrestler, using two hands, grabs his opponent by the belt and carries him out.

TSURITAOSHI (carry down). A wrestler, using two hands, grabs his opponent by the belt and then drops him to the ground.

SOTOGAKE (outside leg trip). A wrestler wraps his leg around the outside of his opponent's and trips him or immobilizes the leg so that the opponent loses balance.

UCHIGAKE (inside leg trip). Similar to *sotogake*, except a wrestler wraps his leg around the inside of his opponent's leg and trips him.

KIRIKAESHI (backward trip). A wrestler places his leg behind his opponent's leg and then pushes or twists him, forcing him to fall backward.

TSUKIDASHI (thrust out). Alternating arms at a very quick pace, a wrestler thrusts blows at his opponent's chest, forcing him out.

OSHIDASHI (push out and down). Using one or two arms, a wrestler forcefully pushes out his opponent.

UTTCHARI (twist out). A wrestler pushed to the edge and nearly out grabs his opponent and, in a desperate move, twists and pushes his opponent out first.

KIMEDASHI (lock and push out). A wrestler locks his arms around his opponent's and forces him out.

ISAMIASHI (accidental step-out). A wrestler on the verge of winning accidentally steps out first.

If a match goes on for a long time and both rikishi appear tired (and have stopped making offensive moves), a gyoji may call a time-out known as *mizu-iri*. He stops the wrestlers in their positions and lets them return to their corners for a brief water break. They then come back to the ring and assume their original positions. The gyoji starts them fighting again by simultaneously hitting the backs of their *mawashi*.

Immediately after the match, the gyoji will point his *gunbai* in the direction of the winning wrestler's side. Sometimes, however, the wrestlers fall at almost the same instant and it is difficult to clearly determine the winner. Even if the result appears to be a tie, the gyoji must still declare one of the wrestlers a winner. If there is any disagreement, the five shinpan (judges) that are seated around the ring will call a *mono-ii* (conference) and enter the ring. There they discuss the match and can either:

1. affirm the referee's decision (*gunbai-dori*)

2. overrule it (*sashichigai*)

3. order a rematch (*torinaoshi*)

In the makuuchi division, an instant video replay of a bout is viewed and the findings are relayed through an earphone to one of the judges. After a decision is reached, the head shinpan announces the result through the PA system for the audience. The conclusion of the judges, not the gyoji, becomes the final decision. No decisions can be reversed at a later time.

POST-BOUT RITUALS

After the match, both wrestlers take their places opposite each other in the ring and bow. Whether a rikishi has won or lost, he is supposed to restrain his emotions. The loser departs the ring, but the winner remains, squatting, as the referee brings over the envelopes containing the *kensho-kin* (encouragement money) on his *gunbai*. Before taking the envelopes the wrestler expresses thanks to the gods by chopping his right hand over the envelopes back and forth, three times, a gesture called *tegatana o kiru* (using the hand to cut like a sword). If there are no envelopes, the wrestler thanks the gods by swinging his right hand through the air in one swift motion. With or without *kensho-kin*, the wrestler then exits the *dohyo* and waits in the corner to give *chikara mizu* to the next fighter from his side.

The victorious wrestler gives thanks by chopping his right hand three times over the money envelopes.

The winning wrestler gives *chikara mizu* to the next fighter.

In the Ring

Sumo bouts are quick, high-powered action! Most matches are over within a few seconds from the moment the wrestlers burst from the tachiai.

The wrestler who falls to the ground or steps or is pushed out of the ring first is the loser of the match. In case of a dispute as to which wrestler won, the shinpan will gather in the center of the ring in a mono-ii, or discussion (see the photo immediately below). The gyoji may not enter the discussion unless he is invited to do so by the shinpan.

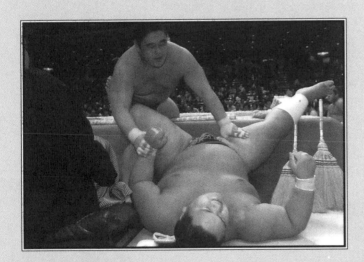

YUMITORI-SHIKI:
THE BOW-TWIRLING CEREMONY

A wrestler in the makushita division is selected to perform the *yumitori-shiki,* or bow-twirling ceremony. The *yumitori-shiki* dates back to the 1700s, when Yokozuna Tanikaze was given a bow as a prize for winning a tournament and, in his happiness, began to twirl the bow around. Nowadays, the ceremony is performed at tournaments and exhibitions following the last makuuchi match of the day. The rikishi enters the *dohyo* from the same side as the winner of the final match and is handed a bow by the gyoji. He then sweeps the bow before him and rapidly twirls it in front of and over his head. If he should happen to drop the bow during the ceremony, he must pick it up with his feet and then continue with the routine; as in the wrestling matches, a hand touching the ground is considered defeat.

The *yumitori-shiki* is considered a gesture of appreciation on behalf of the victorious wrestlers of the day. The wrestler who performs the ceremony is not yet a sekitori, but he wears a *kesho-mawashi* and has his hair done in the fancy *oichomage* style, both normally reserved for the upper-division wrestlers. Although there is a bit of a jinx attached to doing the *yumitori-shiki* (very few performers have reached the sekitori level), the wrestler does receive a cash bonus for his appearance. The performer of the *yumitori-shiki* is generally a wrestler from the same stable (or an affiliate stable) as a yokozuna.

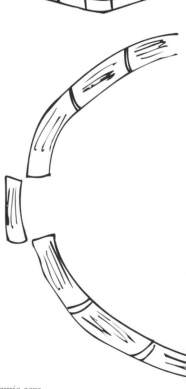

The yumitori-shiki *is a dynamic ceremony that takes a great deal of practice to perform.*

78

No matter which wrestler does the *yumi-tori-shiki*, he always wears the *kesho-mawashi* displaying the decorative crest of the Sumo Association.

SENSHURAKU: THE FINAL DAY

The last day of a tournament is called *senshuraku*. On this day the winner of the tournament is announced and awards and prizes are given. If there is a tie following the upper-division wrestlers' bouts, a *kettei-sen* or playoff will be held to decide the championship. (Playoffs for the lower divisions are held before the makuuchi *dohyo-iri*.) If two rikishi are tied, there is a sudden-death deciding bout. If three rikishi are tied, one wrestler must beat the other two in a row. If there are more than four wrestlers tied, a random draw is made for the playoff. A playoff is the only occasion when rikishi from the same stable can fight each other during a tournament.

Before the last three bouts of the makuuchi division on *senshuraku*, the last three scheduled wrestlers perform the *sanyaku soroi-bumi* ceremony. The East side goes first. The wrestlers align themselves according to rank and clap their hands and stomp their feet in unison. The winner of the third-to-last bout receives an arrow in addition to any *kensho-kin*. The next to last receives a bowstring. The winner of the last match receives a bow.

AWARDS AND PRIZES

After winning the tournament, the new champion goes to his dressing room and has his hair done while answering questions from the press. He then walks down the east *hanamichi* toward the *dohyo*. After the Japanese national anthem is played, the chairman of the Sumo Association gives a short speech and presents the winner with the Tenno-hai or championship trophy. There are dozens of other awards and prizes as well, including prize money worth $100,000.

Next, the recipients of the three special *sansho* awards make their appearance. These awards honor Technique, Fighting Spirit, and Outstanding Performance. Generally, the Technique Award is considered the most prestigious. To qualify for one of these awards, a wrestler must have had a winning record for the tournament (at least 8–7) and be in the makuuchi division, but below ozeki rank. (Although rare, it is possible to be the winner in two or even all three categories. It is also possible that there will be no winner at all.) Each honored rikishi is presented with a trophy along with prize money.

The entire awards ceremony takes almost an hour. After all the prizes are awarded, a brief ceremony called *teuchi shiki* is held for the new rikishi who have just completed their first tournament. The new rikishi along with a gyoji and the final shinpan of the day all stand in a circle on the *dohyo*, pass around a cup of sake, and clap their hands together.

Sanyaku soroi-bumi: East.

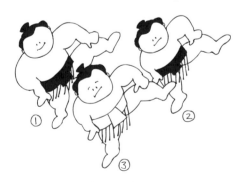

Sanyaku soroi-bumi: West.

Currently, Akinoshima and Kotonishiki have the most *sansho* awards of any active rikishi—fourteen.

THE SPECIAL AWARDS

AWARD NAME	CRITERIA	PRIZE MONEY
Ginosho (Technique Award)	To the wrestler who has displayed exceptional technique	$20,000
Kantosho (Fighting Spirit Award)	To the wrestler who has displayed great fighting spirit and won more matches than usual	$20,000
Shukunsho (Outstanding Performance Award)	To the wrestler who has performed exceptionally well and upset an ozeki, a yokozuna, or the tournament champion	$20,000

The Tenno-hai or Emperor's Cup trophy weighs almost 64 pounds and must be returned the first day of the following tournament. The champion wrestler is given a small replica of the trophy to keep. Kokonoe Oyakata (the ex-yokozuna Chiyonofuji) has all thirty-two of his trophies displayed in a case at his stable.

INCENTIVE PAY

In addition to their salaries, sumo wrestlers receive a form of incentive pay called *mochi-kyukin* or *hoshokin*. Points based on various achievements are accumulated from the moment a wrestler enters the world of sumo (an event worth 3 points) and are thereafter tracked by computer. The rikishi can begin receiving credit in the form of cash for each point after he reaches the juryo division. A wrestler who never reaches juryo may accumulate points but no money. Nothing is ever subtracted from a wrestler's total (thus, if a wrestler has a losing record he simply receives no points). At the end of each tournament, the sekitori's lifetime total of accumulated points is multiplied by 2,500, and the resulting amount is paid out in yen (the figure comes to around $25 for each point).

The amounts generated by the point system can be quite staggering, particularly when you consider that the point total is never diminished and that the money is paid after every tournament, regardless of how well the wrestler performs. (The sekitori is paid even if he misses a tournament

due to illness or injury.) For example, when a maegashira wrestler defeats a yokozuna in a match he is awarded a *kinboshi* (gold star), which is worth 10 points. Thus, for each *kinboshi* he earns, the wrestler is paid a bonus of $250 for the tournament in which he received the *kinboshi* and for every tournament that he competes in thereafter. Akinoshima, a maegashira who in 1997 held the record for most *kinboshi* (fifteen), earns 15 x $250 or an additional $3,750 for every tournament he participates in until he retires from the sport. The opportunity to win a *kinboshi* is obviously a great incentive for maegashira wrestlers to try their best against a yokozuna. See "Sumo Records" on page 136 for a list of wrestlers who have won the most *kinboshi*.

Wrestlers with the record for most *mochi-kyukin* points are:

Taiho	1,491.0
Chiyonofuji	1,447.5
Kitanoumi	1,216.0

Enter sumo	3	Promotion to ozeki	100
Kachikoshi (winning record)	0.5	Promotion to yokozuna	150
Each win over a .500 record	0.5	*Kinboshi* (gold star)	10
Promotion to juryo	40	*Yusho* (win)	30
Promotion to makuuchi	60	*Zensho yusho* (perfect record)	50

After the Tournament

When the awards ceremony is over, the champion returns to the dressing room and changes into Japanese formal wear, a haori (jacket) and hakama (pleated trousers). From there he boards a convertible car for a parade through the streets back to his stable. During the drive, a sekitori stablemate proudly carries the championship flag aloft. The others wrestlers also head home, albeit more modestly. Some walk, while others catch a taxi or ride in their personal cars. On the way out of the stadium, many of the wrestlers will stop and sign autographs or take pictures with eager fans. A yobidashi goes up the tower (yagura) outside the arena and plays a taiko drum to signal the end of the day. Parties, called uchiage, are held later in the evening, either at the various stables or at hotels with large banquet facilities. Fan club members generally are invited to the festivities.

THE SUMO CALENDAR

Although the six yearly *honbasho* are the most important for a sumotori (they are the only tournaments that affect rankings), the time in between tournaments is no vacation. The wrestlers are kept busy with special events, charity tournaments, exhibitions, retirement ceremonies, and other obligations. Here's a typical yearly schedule for the world of sumo.

JANUARY

Practice begins on the 2nd (for most stables)

Yokozuna Shingi-Iinkai Keiko Soken (Special Practice for the Yokozuna Committee, Tokyo)

New recruit initial physical check (Tokyo)

Yokozuna *dohyo-iri* at Meiji Shrine (Tokyo)

Torikumi (bout schedule) meeting

Dohyo Matsuri (blessing of the *dohyo*)

HATSU BASHO (Tokyo, 15 days)

Banzuke ranking meeting (3 days after *basho*)

FEBRUARY

Possible *danpatsu-shiki* (retirement ceremony) if there are any qualified retiring wrestlers (Tokyo)

Special Appearance for Setsu-bun (Coming of Spring) Ceremony at various temples

NHK Charity Sumo Tournament and Karaoke Contest (Tokyo)

Fuji TV Japan Sumo Tournament (Tokyo)

Honozumo (dedication) at Yasukuni Shrine (Tokyo)

Wrestlers travel to Osaka

Haru Basho *banzuke* is published (13 days before the start of *basho*)

Rikishi meeting (Osaka)

MARCH

New recruit initial physical check (Osaka)

Torikumi (bout schedule) meeting

Dohyo Matsuri (blessing of the *dohyo*)

HARU BASHO (Osaka, 15 days)

Banzuke ranking meeting (3 days after *basho*)

Honozumo (dedication) at Ise Shrine (Mie Prefecture)

Haru Jungyo (spring exhibition tour, about 15 days, Kansai and Tokai area)

APRIL

Haru Jungyo continues

Honozumo (dedication) at Yasukuni Shrine (Tokyo)

Natsu Basho *banzuke* is published (13 days before the start of *basho*)

Physical examination (Tokyo)

Exhibitions generally try to travel to each prefecture in Japan at least once every three years, with a visit to Okinawa every five years. If you are lucky, a sumo exhibition could come to your town! Recently, wrestlers have been performing annual overseas *jungyo*. In the past, they have traveled to America (Hawaii, Los Angeles, San Jose, San Francisco, Chicago, and New York), the Soviet Union (Moscow), China (Beijing and Shanghai), Mexico (Mexico City), France (Paris), Brazil (Sao Paulo), England (London), Spain (Madrid), Germany (Dusseldorf), Hong Kong, and Vienna. Australian and Canadian tours are also planned.

MAY

Yokozuna Shingi-Iinkai Keiko Soken (Special Practice for the Yokozuna Committee, Tokyo)

New recruit initial physical check (Tokyo)

Rikishi meeting (Tokyo)

Torikumi (bout schedule) meeting

Dohyo Matsuri (blessing of the *dohyo*)

NATSU BASHO (Tokyo, 15 days)

Banzuke ranking meeting (3 days after *basho*)

JUNE

Possible *danpatsu-shiki* if there are any qualified retiring wrestlers (Tokyo)

Nihon TV Sumo Tournament (Tokyo)

Possible overseas *jungyo* (varies year to year)

Wrestlers travel to Nagoya

Nagoya Basho *banzuke* is published (13 days before the start of *basho*)

Rikishi meeting (Nagoya)

JULY

New recruit initial physical check (Nagoya)

Torikumi (bout schedule) meeting

Dohyo Matsuri (blessing of the *dohyo*)

NAGOYA BASHO (Nagoya, 15 days)

Banzuke ranking meeting (3 days after *basho*)

Natsu Jungyo (summer exhibition tour, about 25 days, Hokuriku and Hokkaido area)

AUGUST

Natsu Jungyo continues

Aki Basho *banzuke* is published (13 days before the start of *basho*)

Physical examination (Tokyo)

Rikishi meeting (Tokyo)

SEPTEMBER

Yokozuna Shingi-Iinkai Keiko Soken (Special Practice for the Yokozuna Committee, Tokyo)

New recruit initial physical check (Tokyo)

Dohyo Matsuri (blessing of the *dohyo*)

AKI BASHO (Tokyo, 15 days)

Banzuke ranking meeting (3 days after *basho*)

TV Asahi Charity Sumo (Tokyo)

All-Japan Sumo Tournament (Tokyo)

OCTOBER

Possible *danpatsu-shiki* if there are any qualified retiring wrestlers (Tokyo)

Aki Jungyo (fall exhibition tour, about 15 days, western and southern Japan)

Chunichi Newspaper Sumo Playoff Tournament (Nagoya)

Kyushu Basho *banzuke* is published (13 days before the start of *basho*)

Rikishi meeting (Fukuoka)

NOVEMBER

New recruit initial physical check (Fukuoka)

Torikumi (bout schedule) meeting

Dohyo Matsuri (blessing of the *dohyo*)

KYUSHU BASHO (Fukuoka, 15 days)

Banzuke ranking meeting (3 days after *basho*)

DECEMBER

Fuyu Jungyo (winter exhibition tour, about 20 days, Kyushu)

Hatsu Basho *banzuke* is published (16 days before the start of *basho*)

Physical examination (Tokyo)

Rikishi meeting (Tokyo)

Hanazumo

All sumo events, except for the six main basho, are called hanazumo, or "flower sumo." During these special events, such as a danpatsu-shiki (retirement ceremony) or a jungyo (exhibition tour), a spectator can enjoy many aspects of sumo that can't be seen during a tournament (at one of the early American tours in the 1960s, there was talk about having the wrestlers wear boxer shorts under their mawashi so as not to offend the nudity-conscious Americans; fortunately, the promoters decided to keep the exhibition authentic and allowed the wrestlers to wear only their mawashi). This page, clockwise from top: a yokozuna challenging five wrestlers; an interview with top gyoji; a demonstration of how a yokozuna tsuna (belt) is tied on; special rikishi introductions; top-ranked wrestlers practicing together.

86

This page, clockwise: sandan-gamae *(a ceremony involving two yokozuna)*; a yobidashi *(ring attendant) giving a drumming demonstration;* sanyaku soroi-bumi, *performed by the three top-ranked wrestlers on each side, normally seen only on the last day of a tournament; children challenging top wrestlers; wrestlers performing* sumo jinku *(sumo songs; many wrestlers are known for their skill at karaoke, and Konishiki and Daishi are among the very best); a demonstration of how a* tokoyama *(hairdresser) prepares a wrestler's hair;* shokkiri, *or comic sumo; interviews with top wrestlers.*

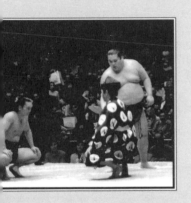

SHIKONA: FIGHTING NAMES

The custom of *shikona*, or fighting names, dates back to the mid-1500s. *Ronin*, or masterless samurai who were no longer attached to a lord, gave themselves strong-sounding names to instill fear in opponents as well as to hide their true identity. Today, many sumo wrestlers debut under their own names and eventually adopt a *shikona*. Very few, such as the former yokozuna Wajima, keep their real names throughout their career. Usually the oyakata, okamisan (the stablemaster's wife), a coach, or even a sponsor try to think of an appropriate *shikona* for the wrestler. The wrestler himself has no say in picking his fighting name.

A *shikona* can be taken from a location (for example a wrestler's home town), nature, strong images, part of the oyakata's or stable's name, or even part of the wrestler's real name. Long-held stable names are usually passed down to star-potential recruits. For example, the present Konishiki's name came from Takasago-beya's yokozuna of the 1890s. Often, names are changed upon promotion. The present Takanohana first fought under the name Takahanada. Upon his promotion to ozeki in 1993 his name was changed to Takanohana, which was passed down to him from his father (who had made ozeki under the same name). The present Wakanohana, whose name comes from his uncle, a former yokozuna, made his debut as Wakahanada and also changed his name upon promotion to oze-ki. Sometimes an oyakata will change a wrestler's name in the hope that the new name will give the rikishi more power to rise in the ranks. Such was the case with Akebono (Dawn) whose original *shikona* was Daikai (Great Sea).

Each stable has its own style and tradition for selecting a wrestler's name. For example, because Azumazeki Oyakata's

fighting name was Takamiyama, several wrestlers in his stable have *shikona* that begin with the same two characters *taka* (high) and *mi* (see):

 Takamihana, Takamiazuma, Takamio, Takaminobori, Takamimaru, Takamishin, Takamisano, Takamiwaka

Similarly, the oyakata of Futagoyama-beya is the former Takanohana, and many of his wrestlers have names that begin with the character *taka* (noble):

 Takanohana, Takanonami, Takatoriki , Takanohikari, Takanoumi, Takayamamoto, Takanosho, Takaibuki, Takanonada, Takanomori

Most of the wrestlers from Oshima-beya have names that start with the character that can be read as *kyoku* or *asahi* (morning sun), such as:

Asahiyutaka, Asahisato, Kyokushuzan, Kyokutenho, Kyokugozan, Kyokuryuzan, Kyokubenten, Kyokukoyama, Kyokutenzan, Kyokuhikari

All wrestlers from Sadogatake-beya have names that start with *koto* (a zitherlike Japanese musical instrument):

 Kotonishiki, Kotonowaka, Kotoinazuma, Kotobeppu, Kotoryu, Kotogaume, Kotokanyu, Kotoarashi, Kotoasaki, Kotonomine

Some of the rikishi from Kokonoe-beya, whose oyakata is the former Chiyonofuji, are given a *shikona* that begins with the characters *chiyo*:

千代 Chiyotaikai, Chiyonowaka, Chiyonosho, Chiyotenzan, Chiyononada, Chiyotenma, Chiyonokuni, Chiyonomori, Chiyonohana, Chiyonomai, Chiyohikari, Chiyofuki

Although all *shikona* are written with *kanji* characters that represent objects or ideas, most Japanese do not think of their literal meanings. However, here are some English equivalents for the more common *kanji* characters used in wrestlers' fighting names:

yama	mountain	*umi*	sea, ocean
nami	wave	*taka*	high, noble
waka	youth	*kuni*	country
ryu	dragon	*asa*	morning
dai	big, great	*fuji*	Mt. Fuji
hana	flower	*nishiki*	brocade
kita	north	*shima*	island
koto	Japanese zither	*riki*	strength, power
asahi	morning sun	*sakura*	cherry blossom
yutaka	abundance	*ten*	sky, heavens

When you become familiar with the common *shikona*, you can put together the literal meanings of the names some of today's popular rikishi:

Akebono = Dawn

Takanohana = Noble Flower

Wakanohana = Young Flower

Musoyama = Mountain of Musashi

Takanonami = Noble Wave

Naminohana = Wave of Flower

Konishiki = Little Brocade

Kotonishiki = Koto of Brocade

Kotonowaka = Koto of Youth

Mainoumi = Dancing Ocean

Kotoinazuma = Koto of Lightning

Mitoizumi = Spring of Mito

Oginohana = Flower of Ogi

Dairyu = Big Dragon

Asanowaka = Youth of Morning

Asahisato = Home of the Morning Sun

Asahiyutaka = Abundance of Morning Sun

Tomonohana = Flower of Knowledge

Hamanoshima = Island Beach

Daishi = Great Reach

Akinoshima = Island of Aki

Kenko = Shining Sword

Tochiazuma = East Horse Chestnut

Kyokushuzan = Mountain of the Eagle of the Morning Sun

Sentoryu = Fighting Dragon

Sunahama = Sandy Beach

Daishoho = Great Soaring Phoenix

Takatoriki = Noble Fighting Sword

Asanosho = Soar of Morning

Misugisato = Three Cedars Village

Higonoumi = Sea of Higo

Kotoryu = Koto of Dragon

PHYSICS OF A WRESTLER'S PHYSIQUE

Probably the most frequently asked question about sumo wrestling is "Why are the wrestlers so fat?" Having a big body is obviously advantageous in sumo. Can you imagine trying to move Konishiki, the biggest athlete in the world? To understand the physics of sumo, try this exercise at home (you will need a partner):

1. Stand directly in front of your partner (slightly less than arm's length away).

2. Have your partner push on one of your shoulders.

3. Result: You are probably easy to move and lose your balance.

4. Next: Spread your feet out and crouch down. Now have your partner try to push you.

5. Now what is the result?

You were probably harder to move, right? The reason you were more stable is that crouching lowers your center of gravity, which is where your body's weight is balanced. The lower the center of gravity, the harder it is to fall.

That's why sumo wrestlers eat so much. By having a big stomach, they lower their center of gravity (kind of like a pyramid), giving them better balance. Also, the bigger a wrestler is, the harder it is to move him and the easier it is for him to move you (force = mass x acceleration). This is

clearly demonstrated in the *tachiai*, or initial clash. When a larger wrestler slams into a smaller one, the force causes the smaller one to move backward, immediately putting him at a disadvantage. It can be compared to a locomotive smashing into a bicycle.

Yet when most rookies enter sumo, they weigh less than 200 pounds. The average weight in the top makuuchi division is 335 pounds, so, in most cases, gaining weight is a requirement for advancement. Eating all the food and candy that you want sounds fun, doesn't it? But for the majority of the wrestlers, that isn't the case at all. Sumotori generally do not pig out on junk food, and many of them have trouble gaining the necessary weight. Some almost force themselves to eat to the point of feeling sick. Chowing down large portions of *chankonabe* (a nutritious high-calorie stew, see page 28) along with huge bowls of rice (depending on the wrestler, ten to twenty cups a day!) can help. Some wrestlers consume over 20,000 calories a day. That's ten times more than the average person!

However, coaches advise that weight gain should be kept in proportion to muscle growth. The best formula for a wrestler is to steadily gain weight while going up the ranks (Akebono gained nearly 200 pounds from his debut until he reached yokozuna). Coaches will often not recruit boys who are extremely over-

Kaio, Akebono, and Musashimaru displaying their big bodies.

90

Akebono	6'8"	484 lbs.	Tochiazuma	5'11"	311 lbs.
Takanohana	6'1"	345	Hamanoshima	5'10"	278
Wakanohana	5'10"	279	Terao	6'0"	257
Musashimaru	6'3"	447	Konishiki	6'0"	604
Takanonami	6'5"	379	Yamato	6'2"	419
Kaio	6'0"	334	Mainoumi	5'7"	221
Musoyama	6'0"	375	Daishi	5'11"	378
Kotonishiki	5'9"	310	Kotonowaka	6'3"	384
Asahiyutaka	6'2"	305	Akinoshima	5'9"	335
Takatoriki	5'11"	325	Kenko	6'3"	330
Tosanoumi	6'1"	331	Asanowaka	5'9"	315
Tamakasuga	6'0"	325	Asanosho	6'0"	322
Kyokushuzan	5'11"	275	Dejima	5'10"	325

weight to begin with, since such boys tend to be lazy and not involved in sports, traits incompatible with the competitive and disciplined world of sumo. Instead, young athletes, especially those who have studied martial arts, that are not too tall, and that have the ability to gain weight, are the most sought-after recruits.

Big has its advantages in sumo, but fortunately, for smaller wrestlers like Mainoumi and Kyokushuzan, it is not always better. A large wrestler can use his massive size to bulldoze his opponent, but he will not necessarily win. The secret to sumo, even more important than weight, speed, and strength, is good technique and balance. A large wrestler may be strong and able to push his opponent out of the ring, but if he loses his balance and falls first, he loses the bout. When a big wrestler is pushing, he must lean forward to generate power, thus sacrificing his own balance. If the smaller wrestler has skilled technique and timing, at just the right moment he can sidestep around the big wrestler and pull him down without having to use much force. Mainoumi, one of the smallest wrestlers (5' 7"), weighs only 211 pounds but has beaten the 6-foot, 600-pound Konishiki with this technique. That's the beauty of sumo. For every advantage there is a disadvantage. Consequently, there is a very fine line between executing a winning technique and being the victim of it.

Although even the smaller sumotori are fairly big, don't mistake them for being "fat." Wrestlers do need a layer of fat to absorb the impact of falling, but underneath that soft tissue lies rock-hard muscles. Akebono has a huge stomach, yet it is very firm and doesn't jiggle. Most wrestlers have solid muscular arms and legs like race horses. They are extremely strong yet agile athletes. Some sumo wrestlers actually have a lower body-fat percentage than the average businessman. (When active, former yokozuna Chiyonofuji had only 11 percent body fat; the average person is 13 percent.)

Train hard, eat plenty

Sumotori are large, and so are the everyday objects they use. In addition to wearing XXXL clothes, they have extra-large cups, rice bowls, futons, cars (vans or sport utility vehicles are popular), and toilets. The toilet seats installed in the Kokugikan dressing rooms are 20 inches wide and 23 inches long (over a half foot bigger than standard ones!).

A Noble Strength

There are no weight divisions in sumo, so it is beneficial to be big. But as big as they are, the wrestlers have a great sense of balance and are very flexible and muscular. They are hard working and dignified men who dedicate their lives to this traditional sport.

HEALTH HAZARDS OF BEING A RIKISHI

For the largest sumo wrestlers who gain in excess of 400 pounds, there are some obvious health hazards. Rikishi are regularly checked by doctors during their physical exams several times a year. Making sure that the wrestlers are staying healthy and in shape, and not just gaining weight, is important. Heavy sumotori are prone to diabetes, heart trouble, high blood pressure, weak circulation, and joint injuries (Akebono and Konishiki both have knee problems). Many active wrestlers are hesitant to diet for fear of losing strength, but they are strongly encouraged to do so after they retire. Like the process of gaining weight for a young rikishi, the process of losing weight for a retiring wrestler should also be gradual. Most retired wrestlers are quite successful at shedding the excess pounds.

For active rikishi, the most common sickness is actually the ordinary cold. Most stables are not equipped with heaters, and lower-ranked wrestlers are not allowed to wear coats, only *yukata*, or thin cotton robes. On top of that, the rikishi all live together, practice together, eat together, and even sleep in the same room (only sekitori wrestlers are permitted to have their own rooms), so if one wrestler catches a virus, it can quickly spread to the others.

Although some sumo wrestlers smoke, all are forced to drink. Of course many rikishi enjoy alcohol, but for those that don't the constant imbibing can be a real chore. Wrestlers are always attending parties and events where intoxicating beverages flow freely. In Japanese society, drinking is not only a means of celebration, it is a custom. The minute a sumotori empties his glass, it will be filled for another round of toasts. Refusing to drink is just not acceptable. After years of consuming gallons of sake, many rikishi develop weak livers.

Like all athletes, sumotori are also at risk for sports injuries. Serious career-ending injuries are rare, but rikishi suffer through dislocated shoulders, pulled muscles, ankle sprains, knee injuries, sore backs, broken bones, and cuts and bruises. Despite the lack of formal drug testing, the use of drugs and steroids is rare in the sumo world. And although some rikishi are noted playboys, there has not been a single case of a wrestler contracting AIDS.

To a Westerner, these massive men may look unattractive, but they are revered in Japan. High-ranked wrestlers are national heroes and are as popular as movie stars. Many of them marry beautiful women who are former models, actresses, or television personalities. To the Japanese, the sumo rikishi are humble and dignified warriors, probably the closest thing to modern-day samurai.

A backside view of the biggest sumo wrestler of all time: Konishiki, 604 pounds.

RETIREMENT

For most sumo wrestlers, their short fighting careers end in their early to mid-thirties. Upon retirement, called *intai,* a wrestler must give up his *shikona* or fighting name (unless he was a strong yokozuna and is given the honorary privilege of keeping it) and cut off his *chonmage* or topknot. This haircutting ceremony is called the *danpatsu-shiki.* The day of the ceremony starts off like a typical *hanazumo* event, with bouts between wrestlers, *shokkiri* (comic sumo), a demonstration by a yobidashi, and so on. If the retiring wrestler is a yokozuna, he will perform his last *dohyo-iri.* If there are other active yokozuna-ranked wrestlers, they will be his attendants for the ceremony (this is the only time a yokozuna can act as an attendant). It is quite a grand scene to see three yokozuna, all wearing their white tsuna, step up on the *dohyo* together.

The wrestler will then change into his formal wear of *haori* jacket and *hakama* pleated pants and sit in the middle of the *dohyo.* Assisted by a gyoji and using fancy scissors, selected sekitori, friends, boosters, sponsors, and coaches each cut off a little of the retiring wrestler's hair. If the ceremony is held at the Kokugikan, only men are allowed to cut the retiring

wrestler's hair (women are not allowed to step on the *dohyo,* but they may participate if the wrestler has his ceremony at the basement hall in the Kokugikan, at a hotel, or at his stable).

Because there are usually many people in line, only two or three strands are snipped per person. The oyakata makes the last cut. The *danpatsu-shiki* is a very dramatic and emotional ceremony. Many wrestlers, normally calm and composed, have completely broken down and sobbed. The moment the wrestler's topknot is cut off, he is no longer a rikishi. The wrestler then rises and, together with his oyakata, bows to each of the four sides of the arena. He then retreats to the dressing room, where he changes into a suit and gets his first full haircut since entering sumo. A party is usually held afterward, either in the basement of the Kokugikan or in a hotel banquet room.

In order to have his formal haircutting ceremony held at the Kokugikan in front of fans and supporters, a wrestler must have participated in a minimum of thirty tournaments from the juryo level or above. Lower-ranked wrestlers who do not meet this qualification usually have their topknots cut off at their stables or at a banquet room at the Kokugikan. Except for the wrestler who performs the *yumitori-shiki* (bow-twirling ceremony), retirement is the only time a lower-ranked wrestler can have his hair done in the fancy *oicho-mage* style.

After his fighting career is over, a wrestler can remain connected to the sumo world, or he can quit the sumo world entirely. The most obvious career choice for a top-ranked wrestler is to become an oyakata (stablemaster). To become an oyakata, a wrestler must:

1. be a Japanese citizen

A sponsor cuts the hair of former sekitori Takamisugi during his retirement ceremony.

Former yokozuna Wajima enjoying his post-sumo life by playing a round of golf.

2. have competed in 20 consecutive juryo tournaments, 25 total juryo tournaments, or 1 tournament in the makuuchi division

3. have purchased *toshiyori-kabu* or elder stock (with only 105 stocks available, they are very expensive and extremely difficult to obtain—today, stock is usually sold at $2–4 million; many rikishi, if they can afford it, try to purchase an elder stock while they are still actively wrestling, instead of waiting until retirement)

4. receive permission from his oyakata

5. receive permission from the Sumo Association

6. have two apprentices

There are some exceptions to these rules. For example, if a wrestler is purchasing an elder stock from his own father, he does not need to meet requirement number 2. If a stock isn't available for purchase, a wrestler can borrow one from another wrestler who owns one but is still active (and isn't currently using the stock). This is known as *kari-kabu*. The original owner retains rights

and can take the stock back at any time (and usually does when he is ready to retire). This gives the borrower a little more time to try and find another stock he can purchase.

Former yokozuna Taiho and Kitano-umi did not have to purchase elder stock to become oyakata. Because of their extraordinary careers they were given *ichidai toshiyori-kabu*, or one-generation elder stock, and were allowed to keep their names as elders. However, their names cannot be passed down or sold after their retirement or death. Former yokozuna Chiyonofuji was also offered *ichidai toshiyori*, but he refused it, opting instead to inherit the stable name where he was trained (Kokonoe).

Only yokozuna wrestlers are given extra time (up to five years) to acquire an elder stock. All other wrestlers must purchase one by the time they retire. However, because the availability of stock is limited, many wrestlers are forced to hang on and continue wrestling in the hope an elder stock will become available.

Wrestlers who do not qualify to become oyakata can work as stable coaches, managers, or assistants. The Sumo Association also hires former wrestlers to assist during tournaments and exhibitions by watching the doors, taking tickets, carrying equipment, keeping records, and so forth. These positions are called wakai-mono-gashira and sewanin and are generally held by former juryo or makushita wrestlers. Yet the number of jobs in sumo is limited, and many wrestlers are forced to leave the sumo world entirely. Some open restaurants or become cooks after gaining culinary skills through stable kitchen duty. Others become professional wrestlers, work in construction, go into business or politics, or become regular salaried employees at companies.

Oyakata   **Cook**   **Pro Wrestler**   **Business-man**

THE JAPAN SUMO ASSOCIATION

The Japan Sumo Association, with more than 1,000 employees, is the organization that runs every aspect of professional sumo. The association went through a radical reform in 1957 under the leadership of Tokitsukaze Oyakata, formerly the yokozuna Futabayama. During his tenure were established minimum height/weight requirements, the sumo school for new recruits, the monthly salary system for sekitori, and the retirement age of sixty-five for gyoji and most other positions in the association. Also in 1957, the name of the association was changed to Nihon Sumo Kyokai (Japan Sumo Association).

The most powerful people within the Sumo Association are the elders. Elder posts are voted on every two years (after the January tournament). There is a set number of positions for each group of affiliated stables (*ichimon*):

rijicho	1 "chairman of the board," usually a former yokozuna
riji	up to 10 "directors"
kanji	3 "supervisors"
yakunin taigu	2–3 "executives"

Monthly salaries (elders who are not officers also receive money) vary with position and range from $6,500 to $12,100.

The Sumo Association has seven divisions: General Operations, Tournaments outside of Tokyo (Osaka, Nagoya, Fukuoka), Exhibition Tours, Training, Judging, Security, Personal Guidance

The Sumo Association has five committees: Sumo Training School (for new recruits), Judging Public Injuries, Physical Examinations, Sumo Museum, Public Relations

NUMBER OF ASSOCIATION POSITIONS

105 toshiyori (elders)

over 800 rikishi (number not fixed)

45 gyoji (referees)

45 yobidashi (ring attendants)

50 tokoyama (hairdressers)

8 sewanin and 8 wakai-monogashira (staff assistants)

about 30 office workers

ICHIMON: AFFILIATED STABLES

An *ichimon* is a group of affiliated stables. Although there are a total of 105 elder names, currently there are only forty-nine active stables divided into five *ichimon*. (Many oyakata do not have the finances or desire to run a stable and thus decide to coach at an already established one.) Stables in the same *ichimon* are encouraged to support each other. For example, if a sekitori wrestler is promoted to a high rank or if he marries or retires, the other ranked wrestlers and coaches from his *ichimon* are expected to attend his celebration. If a yokozuna needs an attendant for the *dohyo-iri* ceremony or a new belt, *ichimon* wrestlers are called on to help.

In earlier times, wrestlers from the same *ichimon* did not have to face each other during tournaments. This rule was changed in 1965 so that now it is only wrestlers from the same stable who are exempt from fighting each other.

Here are the five *ichimon* and their affiliated stables:

出羽海
DEWANOUMI

Total number of elder names: 24

Currently active stables: Dewanoumi, Kasugano, Mihogaseki, Tamanoi, Musashigawa, Kitanoumi, Irumagawa, Hatachiyama

立浪•伊勢ヶ賓
TATSUNAMI / ISEGAHAMA

Total number of elder names: 21

Currently active stables: Tatsunami, Tomozuna, Oshima, Takashima, Toyama, Asahiyama, Ajigawa, Isegahama, Onaruto, Miyagino, Kise, Kiriyama

高砂
TAKASAGO

Total number of elder names: 14

Currently active stables: Takasago, Kokonoe, Takadagawa, Azumazeki, Wakamatsu, Nakamura, Hakaku

二所ノ関
NISHONOSEKI

Total number of elder names: 29

Currently active stables: Nishonoseki, Futagoyama, Sadogatake, Hanakago, Taiho, Kataonami, Oshiogawa, Oguruma, Magaki, Naruto, Minezaki, Hanaregoma, Araiso, Matsugane, Onomatsu

時津風
TOKITSUKAZE

Total number of elder names: 19

Currently active stables: Tokitsukaze, Izutsu, Tatsutagawa, Isenoumi, Shikihide, Kabutoyama, Michinoku, Kagamiyama, Minato

SHINPAN: JUDGES

The shinpan are the five judges who sit on cushions at ringside. There are twenty shinpan, elected for two-year terms. The positions are distributed among the *ichimon.* All shinpan are former wrestlers who are currently oyakata. Wearing the traditional Japanese *haori* and *hakama*, they sit at eye-level to the *dohyo* and watch the action. The judge who sits on the front north side (facing the gyoji straight on) is the *shinpan bucho* (chief judge). In case of a *mono-ii* (conference following a dispute), he listens to an earphone connected to the instant replay room. There, other judges carefully watch the video replay in slow motion and then relay the findings to the chief judge. After the *mono-ii*, the chief judge announces the final decision to the audience. It is the shinpan's decision, not the gyoji's, that is final. Across from the chief judge on the south side are two more judges. The one on the left (on the red tassel side) is the *tokei-gakari* (timekeeper). He signals to the gyoji when the pre-bout ritual time has expired. The remaining two judges sit on the east and west sides in between the wrestlers. A shinpan can stop the action if he feels a false start (*matta*) occurred and can call a *mono-ii* to question a gyoji's close call.

Currently, several former yokozuna serving as shinpan include Kokonoe Oyakata (formerly Chiyonofuji), Sadogatake Oyakata (Kotozakura), Musashigawa Oyakata (Mienoumi), Kitanoumi Oyakata (Kitanoumi), Naruto Oyakata (Takanosato), Magaki Oyakata (Wakanohana II), and Ajigawa Oyakata (Asahifuji).

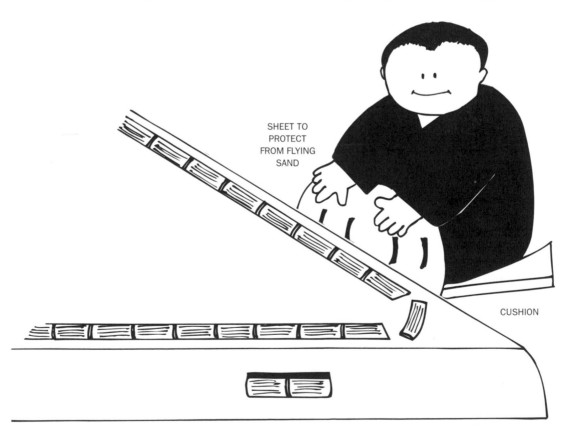

SHEET TO
PROTECT
FROM FLYING
SAND

CUSHION

GYOJI: REFEREES

The Sumo Association employs a total of forty-five gyoji, or referees. As with everything else in sumo, the gyoji have a strict hierarchical system. Most gyoji enter the sumo world after graduating from junior high school. They are affiliated with a stable and usually live there with the wrestlers until they marry. Since there is no such thing as a "referee school," knowledge about refereeing is passed down from a senior to an apprentice.

A new gyoji starts out at the lowest level and gradually works his way up through the ranks. Advancement is very slow; in many cases it takes over fifteen years to reach the juryo level, and probably over forty years to reach the very top. Unlike the wrestlers, who are promoted or demoted after every tournament, referees are promoted only once a year and can never be demoted. Ability along with seniority are the key factors. Because there are only forty-five positions available and the speed of advancement is slow, some gyoji never even reach the makuuchi rank.

THE GYOJI'S ROLE DURING A BOUT

The gyoji enters the ring with the wrestlers and announces their names in a specially trained voice. He directs the wrestlers with commands and with his *gunbai,* or war paddle. When he stands facing forward and holding the *gunbai* out, it signals that the pre-bout time is up and that the wrestlers must begin their match. He carefully watches the *tachiai,* or initial clash, and makes sure that

Top gyoji Kimura Shonosuke.

The gyoji's salary and his costume (*hitatare*) are dependent on rank. The two tate gyoji also carry a small sword in their obi. The gyoji's hat is called an *eboshi.*

RANK	KIMONO	CHORDS	FOOTWEAR
Jonokuchi–Makushita	cotton, tied with a chord below knees	blue or black	barefoot
Juryo	silk, full length	blue and white	*tabi*
Makuuchi	silk, full length	red and white	*tabi*
Sanyaku	silk, full length	red	*setta* and *tabi*
Tate gyoji (Shikimori Inosuke)	silk, full length	purple and white	*setta* and *tabi*
Tate gyoji (Kimura Shonosuke)	silk, full length	purple	*setta* and *tabi*

MADA, MADA! MADA, MADA!
MADA, MADA! MADA, MADA!
MADA, MADA! KAMAETE!
KAMAETE! KAMAETE!
KAMAETE! KAMAETE! MATTA
NASHI! MATT   ASHI! MATTA
NASHI! MA   ASHI! TE O
TSUITE! T   UITE! TE O
TSUITE! T   UITE! TE O
TSUITE!   KOTTA!
NOKOT   NOKOTTA!
NOKO   KKEYOI!
HAKK   KKEYOI!
HAKKE   OI! MADA,
MADA!   A,   A! MADA,
MADA! MADA, MADA! MADA,
MADA! KAMAETE! KAMAETE!
KAMAETE! KAMAETE!
KAMAETE! MATTA NASHI!
MATTA NASHI! MATTA NASHI!
MATTA NASHI! TE O TSUITE!

A GYOJI'S COMMANDS

Mada, mada! = **Not yet, you still have time!**

Kamaete! = **Get ready, take your positions!**

Matta nashi! = **Time is up!**

Te o tsuite! = **Put your hands down!**

Nokotta, nokotta! = **You're still in!**

Hakkeyoi! = **Do something! Get going!**

both wrestlers touch the ground with their hands and start at the same time. During the bout, he repeatedly shouts out, "*Nokotta, nokotta, nokotta!*" (You're still in!) or "*Hakkeyoi!*" (Do something, get going!). After the match, the gyoji must declare the winner by immediately pointing his *gunbai* toward the victorious wrestler's side.

All referees, according to custom, adopt a "sumo" name, either Kimura or Shikimori. Originally Kimura and Shikimori were two families of gyoji; the bloodline has been lost, but the names live on. In a tournament, when announcing the wrestlers' names, a Kimura referee will keep his palm facing downward when he holds the *gunbai.* A Shikimori referee will keep his palm facing upward. There are two tate gyoji, or chief referees. The senior tate gyoji, who only officiates the last match of the day, is always called Kimura Shonosuke (the name, along with a 140-year-old *gunbai,* is passed down from each senior referee to his successor). The junior tate gyoji is always called Shikimori Inosuke.

Only tate gyoji are allowed to judge matches when a yokozuna is fighting. They keep a small sword, or *taisho,* in their obi as a reminder that a gyoji who makes a mistake in judgment should commit *seppuku* (ritual self-disembowelment). Of course, this is only a cautionary symbol; a *tate-gyoji* who happens to make an error will usually turn in his resignation papers instead. Although the gyoji's resignation is generally not accepted, the gesture does show the importance of the job. In addition to working the matches, gyoji also keep records, act as announcers, and write the daily tournament schedule (*torikumi-hyo*) and *banzuke* in the fancy calligraphy style known as *sumo-moji.* High-ranking gyoji also bless the *dohyo* in a ceremony prior to each tournament. The mandatory retirement age for a gyoji is sixty-five.

The lifestyle of a gyoji is so strict that half of the new recruits quit within the first year.

A gyoji goes barefoot in the ring until he reaches the juryo rank. At that time, he is finally allowed to wear *tabi*, or Japanese-style socks. The *tabi* are made to be worn indoors on tatami, not on a rough and sandy surface like the *dohyo*. Consequently, a gyoji will go through several pairs each tournament. A gyoji must reach the sanyaku rank before he is allowed to wear *setta*, Japanese-style slippers.

101

YOBIDASHI: RING ATTENDANTS

Yobidashi, or ring attendants, are considered the busiest people in sumo. There are forty-five of them, all employed by the Sumo Association but affiliated with a stable. As with the gyoji, everything is taught to a young yobidashi by a senior. Yobidashi are ranked and listed on the *banzuke*:

1. Tate-yobidashi
2. Fukutate-yobidashi
3. Sanyaku-kaku
4. Makuuchi-kaku
5. Juryo-kaku
6. Makushita-kaku
7. Sandanme-kaku
8. Jonidan-kaku
9. Jonokuchi-kaku

The retirement age for a yobidashi is sixty-five. Here are some of the jobs a yobidashi is responsible for:

construction of the *dohyo* (for tournaments and practice areas)

It is said that it takes a yobidashi two years to learn how to make the right sound with the wooden clappers, and ten years to learn to recognize the correct type of clay used in constructing the dohyo.

beating drums around the Ryogoku neighborhood prior to each Tokyo tournament (to announce the upcoming *basho*)

during tournaments, calling out the wrestler's name in a specially trained, reedy voice

clapping two wood blocks together during the *dohyo-iri* announcements (it takes years of practice to consistently get the right sound)

refilling the salt baskets by the *dohyo*

helping the rikishi with power water (*chikara mizu*) and power paper (*chikara gami*)

handing small towels to the wrestlers to use during pre-bout rituals

laying out each sekitori's cushion

sweeping the *dohyo* before every match

circling the *dohyo* with the *kensho-kin* (encouragement money) flags

folding the winning rikishi's *sagari* and attaching the winning *kensho-kin* money envelopes together

selling books and brochures in a shop at the Kokugikan

bringing out the awards on the last day

playing the *taiko* drum in the tower outside of the arena to signal the end of the day, a performance called *yaguradaiko*

writing sumo songs

Some yobidashi are very skilled poets and songwriters. They write *sumo jinku*, songs that describe the hardships a wrestler goes through, celebrate the promotion of a wrestler, or congratulate a retiring wrestler on a glorious career. Songs written by yobidashi are often performed at *jungyo* (exhibitions) by sumo wrestlers.

HIGAAAAAA~~~~SHIIIIIII ~~~~

NIIIIIIIIII ~~~~SHIIIIIIIII ~~~~

HIGAAAAAA~~~~SHIIIIIII ~~~~

NIIIIIIIIII ~~~~SHIIIIIIIII ~~~~

HIGAAAAAA~~~~SHIIIIIII ~~~~

NIIIIIIIIII ~~~~SHIIIIIIIII ~~~~

HIGAAAAAA~~~~SHIIIIIII ~~~~

NIIIIIIIIII ~~~~ IIIIII ~~~~

HIGAAAA ~IIIIII ~~~~

NIIIIIIIIII ~~ III ~~~~

HIGAAAA IIIII ~~~~

NIIIIIIIIII ~~ III ~~~~

HIGAAAAA~ SHIIIIII ~~~~

NIIIIIIIIII ~~ IIIIII ~~~~

HIGAAAAAA~ ~SHIIIIIII ~~~~

NIIIIIIIIII ~~ IIIIIII ~~~~

HIGAAAAAA~~~~SHIIIIIII ~~~~

NIIIIIIIIII ~~~~SHIIIIIIIII ~~~~

HIGAAAAAA~~~~SHIIIIIII ~~~~

NIIIIIIIIII ~~~~SHIIIIIIIII ~~~~

HIGAAAAAA~~~~SHIIIIIII ~~~~

NIIIIIIIIII ~~~~SHIIIIIIIII ~~~~

TOKOYAMA: HAIRDRESSERS

Three hundred years ago, the topknot or *chonmage*, was the normal hair style for males in Japan. After the Meiji Restoration of 1868, the government ordered men, with the exception of sumo wrestlers, to modernize their appearance by cutting off their *chonmage* and wearing short Western-style hair cuts. In time, the hairdressers who knew how to prepare the *chonmage* almost disappeared, and hairdressers from the costumed Kabuki theater, called tokoyama, were borrowed to do the hair of sumo wrestlers. Today, many stables have their own tokoyama. Those without either borrow one from another stable, or during tournaments wrestlers can have their hair done at the arena. There are fifty tokoyama in all.

All sumo wrestlers have their hair done in the traditional *chonmage*, except for the rookies, whose hair is too short to have it put up in a topknot. Upon entering the sumo world, a recruit will stop cutting his hair. When the bangs in the front and the hair from the back can come around and touch the chin; it will be long enough

to be fixed in a topknot. The first time a rikishi has his hair done in a *chonmage* is usually a memorable event. Most comment that afterward they at last feel like a real sumotori.

In his everyday life, whether practicing or going out, a wrestler wears his hair in the simple topknot. When he reaches the sekitori level, during tournaments he wears his hair in the more elaborate *oichomage* style, which resembles a ginkgo leaf. This fancy style is also worn on special occasions, such as when the wrestler is promoted, marries, or retires.

All tokoyama adopt names that begin with the prefix *Toko-*. The rest of their name could be taken from their real name; thus, a tokoyama's name might be Tokofuji, Tokoken, or Tokokazu. Or it could come from the stable name; the tokoyama Tokoazuma would be from Azumazeki-beya and Tokosado would be from Sadogatake-beya. All hairdressers are affiliated with a stable and ranked in six divisions. Only tokoyama in the top two divisions can prepare the elaborate *oicho-*

When not in a *chonmage*, a wrestler's hair looks very long.

If a wrestler has too much thick hair, it will be difficult to fold the hair over into a topknot, so a tokoyama shaves the top of the head.

mage. It is said that it takes up to ten years to learn how to style it properly using an assortment of different-sized combs, picks, and a special wax called *bintsuke*. Many tokoyama keep a long thumbnail on one hand that they use to shape the *oichomage*. The mandatory retirement age for a hairdresser is sixty-five.

3.

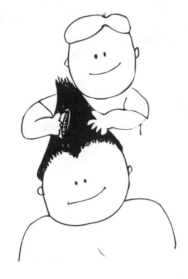

The tokoyama combs out the hair, removing any sand or dirt, and applies *bintsuke*.

4.

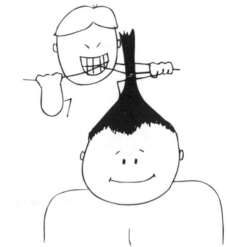

He ties the topknot with white string.

5.

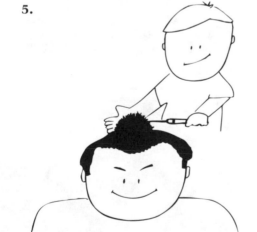

After folding over the topknot, using a pick and his hand he forms the *oichomage*.

6.

A sekitori's *oichomage*.

Hair Care

The chonmage is considered the symbol of a sumo wrestler. Not only does it act as a head protector (a sort of helmet in case of falls), but it's also considered sexually appealing by many women. On this page, Takasago-beya's tokoyama Tokofuji styles American Sunahama's hair before a tournament.

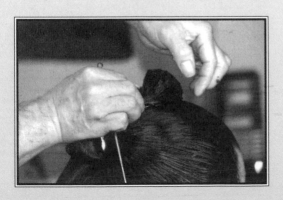

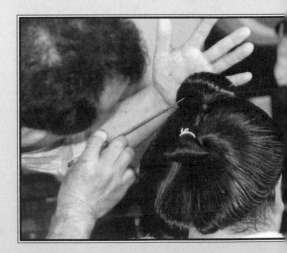

The tokoyama uses bintsuke, similar to butch wax, to help hold the hair in place. Bintsuke has such a pleasant and unique smell that it acts almost like a cologne in attracting women. Even after a sumotori leaves a room, the sweet smell of his hair remains. A wrestler only washes his hair once or twice a week. When he does wash it, it takes almost half a bottle of shampoo to clean it and remove the bintsuke. A tsukebito will scrub a sekitori's hair and clean it for him.

Regular chonmage.

Fancy oichomage.

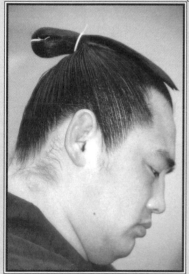

107

VISITING RYOGOKU

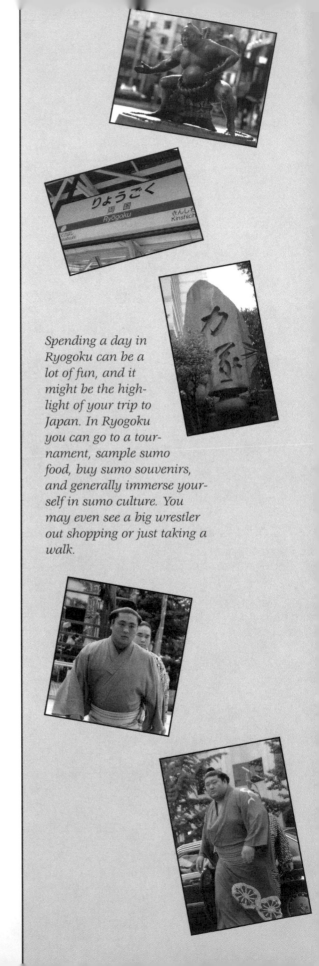

It is very easy to get to Ryogoku by train. Ryogoku Station is just north of downtown on the Sobu Line, which you can reach by taking the JR Yamanote Line that runs in a circular route around central Tokyo, stopping at all the major stations (Shibuya, Harajuku, Shinjuku, Ikebukuro, Ueno, Tokyo, Shinbashi, Shinagawa, and so on). Get off the Yamanote Line at Akihabara Station, which is two stops north of Tokyo Station. Exit down the stairs and then transfer to the yellow Sobu Line, platform number 6, going east toward Chiba. Ryogoku Station is the second stop from Akihabara. Akihabara can also be reached using the Hibiya Line subway, which can be boarded at Ginza, Kamiyacho, and other centrally located stations.

After exiting at Ryogoku, you will be able to see the Kokugikan sumo arena on the north side. Near the bus terminals are bronze statues with *tegata* (hand prints) of past yokozuna. If you walk toward the west end of the station (toward the arena), behind all of the ticket machines are several life-size portraits of past tournament champions on display. (During tournaments you should buy your return ticket right after arriving at the station. If you wait until 6 pm, you will have to fight the crowds and the lines.)

On tournament days, banners with the names of the makuuchi-division wrestlers will be on display outside the Kokugikan. Although it will be crowded, if you wait by the guarded south gates (to the right of the ticket entrance) you will be able to see the wrestlers live and up close. From 2 to 3:30 pm, juryo and makuuchi wrestlers make their way to the stadium. At 2 pm guards come out and make sure all spectators remain in the area marked off by the brown tiles on the ground (the closest you will be allowed to stand is the third row of brown tiles from the sidewalk).

Spending a day in Ryogoku can be a lot of fun, and it might be the highlight of your trip to Japan. In Ryogoku you can go to a tournament, sample sumo food, buy sumo souvenirs, and generally immerse yourself in sumo culture. You may even see a big wrestler out shopping or just taking a walk.

108

The best place to stand is on the left side, just in front of the south entrance; here you will be able to see wrestlers entering both from the taxi drop-off and from the parking lot. Get there before 2 pm so you can secure a good position with a good view. Do not approach the wrestlers as they are entering (they are very tense before their bouts), but you can take pictures, so have your camera ready! At 4:30, juryo and makuuchi wrestlers start to exit after their matches. If you are quick, you can ask them for autographs before they get into their cars or catch a taxi.

Ozeki and yokozuna enter through a private parking lot in the basement of the stadium.

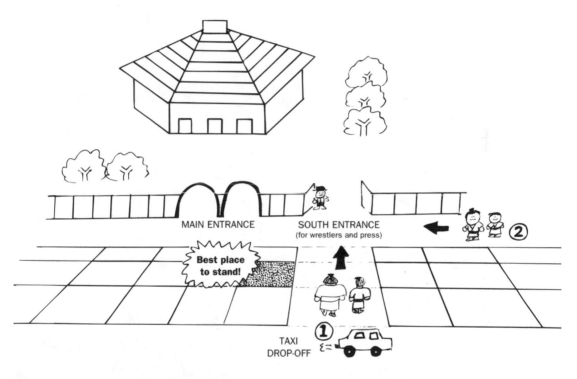

WRESTLERS WHO USUALLY ENTER FROM #1	WRESTLERS WHO USUALLY ENTER FROM #2
Kotobeppu	Akinoshima
Kotonowaka	Asahiyutaka
Mitoizumi	Tokitsunada
Konishiki	Mainoumi
Terao	Daizen
Kotonishiki	Tomonohana
Kenko	Daishoho
Musoyama	Asahiyutaka
Kaio	Takatoriki
Asanowaka	Oginishiki
Kitakachidoki	Tochinowaka
Asanosho	Oginohana
Sunahama	Kyokushuzan

MAP OF RYOGOKU

Ryogoku is the name of the northeastern Tokyo district where the Kokugikan sumo arena and many of the sumo training stables are located. The map here is a rough geographical locator but is not drawn to

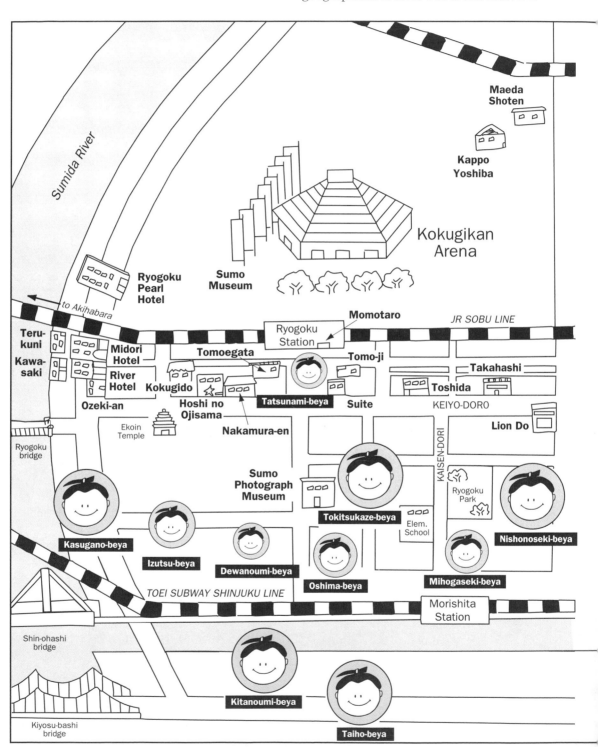

scale. The hotels, restaurants, and shops indicated on the map are described on pages 112–17. The stables shown on the map are those in the "sumo district," and most of the stables in the listings on pages 120–22 are accessible to visitors. More detailed street maps can be obtained at subway stations, bookstores, or for free from offices of the Japan National Tourist Organization near Yurakucho Station.

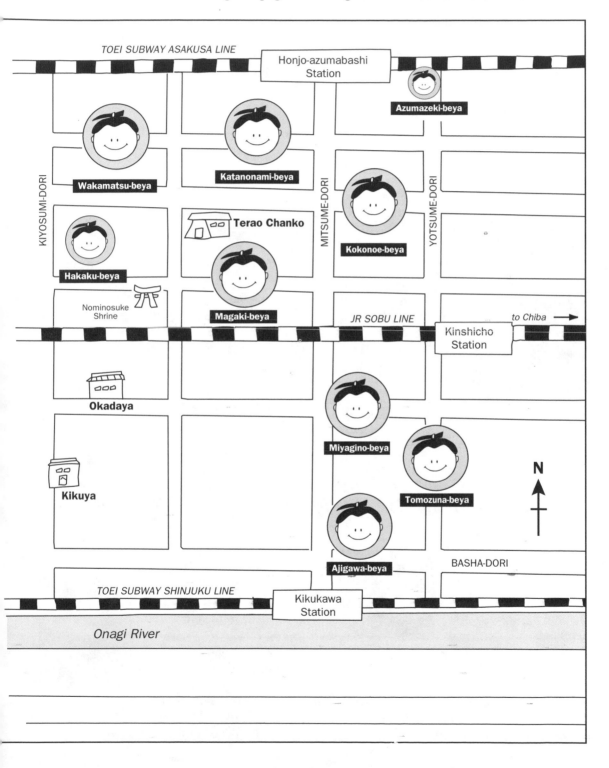

PLACES TO GO

If you are in Ryogoku on a non-tournament day, there's lots to do. First, stop at the Kokugikan to find out more about sumo history.

SUMO MUSEUM
(Sumo Hakubutsukan)

Ryogoku Kokugikan, 1F, 1-3-28 Yokoami, Sumida-ku, Tokyo 130

Open Monday–Friday (during tournaments, only those with tickets may enter)
Hours: 9:30 am–4:30 pm
Phone: 03-3622-0366
Distance: on foot 2 min.

The Sumo Museum is packed with information on the history of sumo. The contents are changed regularly, so you can almost always see something new. English pamphlets are available. Admission is free. Write to the above address for additional information.

SUMO PHOTOGRAPH MUSEUM
(Sumo Shashin Shiryokan)

3-13-2 Ryogoku, Sumida-ku, Tokyo 130

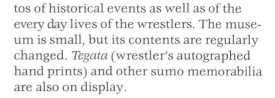

Open regularly only on Tuesdays, every day during Tokyo tournaments
Hours: 10 am–5 pm
Phone: 03-363-2150
Distance: on foot 10 min.

The Sumo Photograph Museum owner's father was a photographer for the Sumo Association during the 1930s. He took photos of historical events as well as of the every day lives of the wrestlers. The museum is small, but its contents are regularly changed. *Tegata* (wrestler's autographed hand prints) and other sumo memorabilia are also on display.

Now, as long as you're in Ryogoku, how about some food? Why not try the meal of sumo wrestlers: *chankonabe*! After all, for a steaming bowl of *chanko*, there is no better place than Ryogoku. There are several *chanko-ya*—restaurants specializing in the tasty stew—within walking distance from the station. Or how about some special sumo cookies or rice crackers? Some original sumo goods? A place to stay overnight? Listed here are the profiles of a few well-known hotels, restaurants, and shops in Ryogoku (see the map on pages 110–11; all distances are measured from Ryogoku Station).

RYOGOKU PEARL HOTEL

1-2-24 Yokoami, Sumida-ku, Tokyo 130

Check in: 3 pm
Check out: 10 am
Daily rates: single $75–$85, double $136, twin $136, triple $174, family $275; Japanese-style room for 4 people $260, for 6 people $360
Phone: 03-3625-8080
Distance: on foot 3 min.

Ryogoku Pearl Hotel has 12 floors, 302 rooms (Western style and Japanese style), and a parking lot. Every room comes with a bath, phone, TV/VCR, and refrigerator. There is also a restaurant in the lobby (breakfast $10, lunch from $10, and dinner from $15).

RYOGOKU RIVER HOTEL

2-13-8 Ryogoku, Sumida-ku, Tokyo 130

Check in: 3:30 pm
Check out: 10 am
Daily rate: single $70–$72,
twin $130–$150, triple
$170; Japanese-style
room for 1 person $75, for
2 people $140, for 3 peo-
ple $180, for 4 people
$220, for 5 people $250
Phone: 03-3634-1711
Distance: on foot 3 min.

Ryogoku River Hotel has 100 rooms (Western style and Japanese style). Every room
has a bath, phone, TV, ventilator, and hair
dryer. A restaurant on the first floor serves
breakfast for $8, lunch from $10, and dinner from $15.

MIDORI HOTEL

2-13-7 Ryogoku, Sumida-ku, Tokyo 130

Daily rates: single $70, double $120, twin
$130, capsule $33
Phone: 03-3635-2626
Distance: on foot 3 min.

Midori Hotel has 7 floors
with business or capsule
rooms. There is a coffee
shop, a Chinese restau-
rant, and a karaoke bar. It
is a small hotel and relatively cheap, so if you just
need a place to sleep it is
adequate.

KAPPO YOSHIBA

(*Chankonabe* restaurant)

2-14-5 Yokoami, Sumida-ku, Tokyo 130

Closed Sunday and holidays
Hours: 5 pm–10 pm
Phone: 03-3623-4480
Distance: on foot 20 min., by taxi about $8

Kappo Yoshiba's building was former
yokozuna Yoshibayama's old stable. The

new owners of the
building turned it
into a restaurant,
leaving the prac-
tice area un-
touched. Many of
the tables are actu-
ally on the *dohyo*
or the *agarizashiki* (raised viewing area).
Although it is a little expensive (dinner is
about $90), the atmosphere is great.

TERAO CHANKO

(*Chankonabe* restaurant)

Maison du Rafine 1F, 2-11-2 Ishihara,
Sumida-ku, Tokyo 130

Closed Tuesday
Hours: 5 pm–10 pm
Phone: 03-3626-7541
Distance: on foot 20 min, by taxi about $10

Terao Chanko is owned and operated by

active rikishi
Terao's older
brother, who was
once a wrestler
himself. Inside are
pictures of Terao
and his brothers
and father (the former Tsurugamine). The
specialties are *shoyu* (soy sauce), *miso* (soybean paste), and *ponzu* (citrus vinegar)
style *chankonabe*. Courses range from $20
to $100.

TOMOEGATA

(*Chankonabe* restaurant)

2-17-6 Ryogoku, Sumida-ku, Tokyo 130

Open every day
Hours: 11:30 am–10 pm
Phone: 03-3633-5600
Distance: on foot 4 min.

Tomoegata was the fighting name of the
ninth Tomozuna Oyakata. He opened the
restaurant, and today his son runs the
operation. Each day the lunch menu serves
a different stable's style of *chankonabe*

(Tomozuna-beya, Kitanoumi-beya, Kokonoe-beya, Takasago-beya, Fujishima-beya, Oshima-beya, and Isegahama-beya). Lunch prices are from $11 to $20. Dinners are more expensive and range from $32 to $90.

MOMOTARO CHANKO
(*Chankonabe* restaurant)

Located in Ryogoku Station

Open every day
Hours: 11:30 am–1:30 pm, 5 pm–10 pm
Phone: 03-3633-9774
Distance: on foot 1 min.

The restaurant is connected to Ryogoku Station, so if you are in a hurry to eat, Momotaro is definitely the closest *chanko-ya*. A single  serving of *tori-chanko* (chicken) is $18, *tsumire chanko* (fish ball) $20, and *yokozuna chanko* $25.

TOMO-JI
(*Chankonabe* restaurant)

3-24-4 Ryogoku, Sumida-ku, Tokyo 130

Closed Sunday and holidays
Hours: 5 pm–10:30 pm
Phone: 03-3631-4889
Distance: on foot 4 min.

Tomo-ji is a small restaurant located near  Tatsunami-beya. For one person, *goma miso aji* (sesame seed and soybean paste) or *ponzu* (citrus vinegar) style *chanko* is $26. The restaurant also serves *sashimi* (maguro and hamachi).

SUITE
(Japanese restaurant)

3-21-2 Ryogoku, Sumida-ku, Tokyo 130

Closed Sunday and holidays
Hours: 5 pm–10 pm
Phone: 03-3631-1880
Distance: on foot 7 min.

 Suite is a high-class restaurant, a little on the expensive side. They serve *chanko* (beef and fish) for $20, and also *kaiseki ryori* (Japanese-style set meals): *sashimi*, *yakizakana* (grilled fish), *soba*, tempura, soup, and dessert. Courses are priced at $55 to $100.

KAWASAKI CHANKO
(*Chankonabe* restaurant)

2-13-1 Ryogoku, Sumida-ku, Tokyo 130

Closed Sunday and holidays
Hours: 5 pm–10 pm
Phone: 03-3631-2529
Distance: on foot 5 min.

A little hideaway on a back street not too far from the arena. Kawasaki Chanko has a nice atmosphere and serves tasty *chanko*. Dinner prices start at around $20 per person.

TERUKUNI CHANKO
(*Chankonabe* restaurant)

1-17-6 Ryogoku, Sumida-ku, Tokyo 130

Open every day
Hours: 5 pm–11 pm (Saturday, Sunday: 12 pm–10 pm)

 Phone: 03-3631-0711
Distance: on foot 4 min.

Terukuni Chanko is a fancy *chanko* restaurant near Ryogoku Station.

A simple *chanko* dinner starts at $26 per person. Their specials are the "Terukuni set" for $42 and the "Terukuni course" for $50. Both include *chanko* with the trimmings.

OZEKI-AN
(noodle shop)

2-14-6 Ryogoku, Sumida-ku, Tokyo 130

Closed Saturday
Hours: 7 am–3 pm, 5 pm–9:20 pm
Phone: 03-3631-0720
Distance: on foot 3 min.

For a quick bite of noodles, Ozeki-an is the place. Conveniently located near Ryogoku Station, it is quite affordable for lunch. It serves all kinds of *soba*, including *tanuki* $5, *zaru* $6, and tempura $9.

TOSHIDA
(Pastry shop)

2-32-19 Ryogoku, Sumida-ku, Tokyo 130

Closed Sunday and holidays
Hours: 9 am–8 pm
Phone: 03-3631-3011
Distance: on foot 10 min.

Toshida's best-selling items are *rikishi monaka* (a soft pastry with *anko*, or sweet bean paste, shaped like a sumo wrestler) and *Ryogoku yaki* (pound cake with *anko*). The most popular among neighborhood sumo wrestlers is a *dorayaki*  (sweet bean-filled bun) called *Gottsuan Desu*. These are all sugary Japanese treats that can be bought in boxed sets, from $6, or as singles for about $1.20. They also sell other types of *manju* (beancakes), sugar candy, fruit jelly, and *o-senbei* (rice crackers).

MAEDA SHOTEN
(*O-senbei* shop)

2-4-12 Yokoami, Sumida-ku, Tokyo 130

Open every day
Hours: 7 am–8 pm
Phone: 03-3623-6656
Distance: on foot 20 min.

Maeda Shoten makes a variety of *o-senbei* (rice crackers) including *katayaki* (hard), *miso ajifumi* (beancurd flavor), and *shiro-yaki* (white). Their best-selling cracker is the *sumo senbei* (a soy-sauce-flavored cracker in the shape of a sumo wrestler). *O-senbei* can be purchased as singles, starting at about $0.70 a piece, or as boxed sets starting at $8.50.

KOKUGIDO
(*O-senbei* shop and sumo goods)

2-17-3 Ryogoku, Sumida-ku, Tokyo 130

Irregular closings
Hours: 9 am–8 pm
Phone: 03-3631-3856
Distance: on foot 3 min.

Kokugido's specialty is *anko-arare* (*o-senbei* with *anko* inside). Boxed sets are from $11 to $33 (singles cannot be purchased). They also have a small selection of sumo goods (towels, chopsticks, pens, etc.).

NAKAMURA-EN
(Tea store)

2-17-14 Ryogoku, Sumida-ku, Tokyo 130

Closed Sunday and holidays
Hours: 9 am–8 pm
Phone: 03-3631-2018
Distance: on foot 7 min.

Nakamura-en has been in Ryogoku for over

eighty years. Ocha (tea) sets run from $5 to $55 and *nori* (seaweed) sets are $10 to $90. Their most popular item is a canister of tea with the names of all sixty-four yokozuna printed on it.

HOSHI NO OJISAMA
(Souvenir store)

2-17-16 Ryogoku, Sumida-ku, Tokyo 130

Open: every day
Hours: 9 am–8 pm, Sunday 10 am–8 pm
Phone: 03-3632-7391
Distance: on foot 7 min.

As a special service during tournaments, if you make a purchase of over $20, Hoshi no

Ojisama gives you a current *banzuke* (ranking sheet); the supply is limited. The shop's most popular item is a stuffed sumo wrestler. They have a friendly staff and a great selection of sumo accessories (even Akebono's mom shopped here!). T-shirts start at $10, pens at $5.

TAKAHASHI FUTON TEN
(Edo and sumo goods)

4-31-15 Ryogoku, Sumida-ku, Tokyo 130

Open every day
Hours: 9 am–8 pm
Phone: 03-3631-2420
Distance: on foot 12 min.

Takahashi probably has the best selection of sumo items. Just to list a few: towels, T-shirts, shorts, trash cans, handkerchiefs, aprons, *noren* (curtains), stickers, pens, erasers, stationery, plates, tea cups, lighters, pillows, postcards, bags,

fans, and much more. Their most popular items are sumo pillows and curtains. For anyone interested in sumo accessories, this store is a definite stop!

LION DO
(Clothing store)

4-30-10 Ryogoku, Sumida-ku, Tokyo 130

Closed Sundays and holidays
Hours: 9:30 am–6:30 pm
Phone: 03-3631-0650
Distance: on foot 12 min.

Lion Do has been serving the wrestlers and public of Ryogoku for over ninety years.

They specialize in sumotori-size cloth-ing (XXXXL). Many wrestlers purchase their clothes here. Smaller rikishi like Hamanoshima wear 3L size, while Ko-

nishiki wears 6L. Their best-selling item is the traditional sumo outfit (T-shirt and short pants) that wrestlers are required to wear in the locker rooms during tourna-ments. They cost about $30 each (smaller sizes are cheaper), and for $2 extra they will embroider your name in English or Japanese. There are a variety of colors that you can choose from for the embroidery. Konishiki uses green and Takanohana likes red. While you are there, check out Ko-nishiki's overalls with a size-64-inch waist!

KIKUYA
(*Tabi* store)

1-9-3 Ryogoku, Sumida-ku, Tokyo 130

Open every day
Hours: 9 am–6 pm
Phone: 03-3631-0092
Distance: on foot 15 min.

Kikuya is one of the few remaining stores in Tokyo that produce handmade, custom-fit *tabi* (traditional Japanese-style socks). Workers at the shop make the *tabi* for the

large-footed sumo wrestlers, who usually buy several pairs at one time (Akebono once ordered twenty-two pairs!). You can buy ready-made *tabi* there or for about $10 more you can custom order a pair. The master, Miyauchi Umeji, who has been making *tabi* for over forty years, claims he can tell a lot about the health of a person just by examining his or her feet. There is a small display in the store explaining the history, procedure, and tools used in making the socks; the outlines of famous rikishi's feet can be viewed as well.

OKADAYA
(*Setta* store)

1-17-10 Ryogoku, Sumida-ku, Tokyo 130

Closed Sundays and holidays
Hours: 9 am–8 pm
Phone: 03-3631-2002
Distance: on foot 13 min.

Okadaya has been selling *setta* (Japanese-style sandals) to sumo wrestlers for over a hundred years. Only wrestlers ranked from the sandanme division and above are allowed to wear these fancy sandals (lower-ranked wrestlers must wear *geta*, or wooden thongs). The sandals here come in a variety  of colors, styles, and prices. Wooden *geta* start from $35, *setta* from $55, and *tatami setta* from $500. Inside you can see a pair of Akebono's size 33 (US: 14 1/2) *setta*.

Remember, it is relatively safe walking around Japan. If you should happen to get lost, most Japanese people are helpful and can point the way back to the station for you. So go out and explore the hometown of sumo! *Tanoshinde ne . . .* Have fun!

VISITING A STABLE

Azumazeki-beya, Takasago-beya, Musashigawa-beya

Visiting a sumo stable gives you the chance to watch wrestlers practice. Three stables with a Hawaiian connection are described in detail here. The most popular stables are listed on pages 120–22. The map on pages 110–11 shows all the sumo stables that are within walking distance from Ryogoku Station. Other stables can be reached by taxi or train. Always phone ahead (in Japanese) to be sure the stable will be open to visitors the day you want to go.

Azumazeki-beya　　東関部屋

Oyakata:	former sekiwake Takamiyama (Jesse Kuhaulua)
Sekitori wrestlers:	Yokozuna Akebono (Chad Rowan), Daiki (Percy Kitapa)
Phone:	03-3625-0033

Azumazeki-beya is small (only about ten wrestlers) and personable. The fancy *kanji* characters for the stable sign outside the front entrance were written by former prime minister Nakasone Yasuhiro. In the hallway is a life-size portrait of Jesse in his *kesho-mawashi* after he won the 1972 Nagoya Basho. There is also a large wooden copy of that tournament's *banzuke* on display. On the Shinto altar in the *keikoba* (practice area) are several pieces of Akebono's yokozuna belt. Each time a new belt is made for him, a small piece is cut off and placed in the altar. If you have the chance (and can speak a little Japanese), say hello to stable manager Karimata. He is a very friendly fellow and will answer any questions with a smile. Because the viewing area is limited and television crews are often filming Akebono, try to go early for a good seat. After practice, you might have the chance to see Jesse's dog or better yet talk to Akebono. If he

The broad back of Azumazeki Oyakata.

doesn't have any appointments, don't be afraid to approach him. He is one of the most easygoing sumo wrestlers of all.

CAUTION: Do not sit on the far right side of the *agarizashiki* (raised viewing area). During practice, wrestlers get pushed back and often fall into this area, smashing anything or anyone that may be in the way.

HOW TO GET THERE: Take the Toei Asakusa Line subway to Honjo-azumabashi Station. Exit up the stairs. You can take a taxi to the stable for about $7, but it's probably faster to walk (only about 10 minutes).

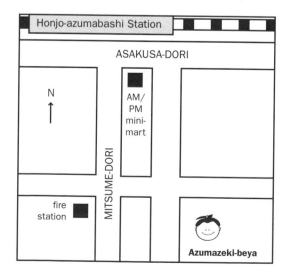

Takasago-beya　　　　　　　　　　高砂部屋

Oyakata:	former komusubi Fujinishiki
Sekitori wrestlers:	Konishiki (Salevaa Atisanoe), Mitoizumi, Sunahama (Tyler Hopkins)
Phone:	03-3876-7770

Takasago-beya is a stable with a long and rich history. It was established in 1878 by Takasago Uragoro. To date, a total of six yokozuna wrestlers have been produced by the stable. Takasago-beya was also the first stable to have a foreign champion wrestler, Takamiyama (Jesse Kuhaulua), who still remains affiliated (in the same group or *ichimon*) through his Azumazeki-beya.

Inside the *keikoba* are pictures of the stable's past oyakata. There are also huge piles of *zabuton* (cushions), so grab a couple to sit on and make yourself comfortable while you watch practice. After the

daily workout is over, lower-ranked wrestlers clean and hang out the *mawashi* to dry over the three-story building. As you are leaving, you might want to stop by Asakusa

Hawaiian wrestler Koryu relaxing after practice.

Kaminarimon. It is a large temple with dozens of small shops selling all kinds of souvenirs. A major tourist attraction in Japan, it is only a 2-minute walk from the station.

CAUTION: Do not try and talk to Takasago Oyakata during practice (or complain about his cigarette smoke). He is a very serious man.

The viewing area at Takasago-beya.

HOW TO GET THERE: You can catch either the Toei Asakusa Line subway or the Ginza Line subway to Asakusa Station. Exit up the stairs to the street level and catch a taxi to the stable (the fare is around $10). If you decide to walk, it will take about 20 minutes.

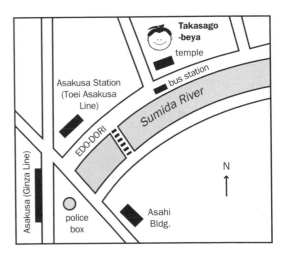

Takasago-beya is almost considered the "Hawaii connection." It is the stable that recruited the first successful American, Takamiyama (Jesse Kuhaulua). Takasago-beya also produced the first foreign ozeki, Konishiki (Salevaa Atisanoe). Along with Konishiki, juryo-ranked wrestler Sunahama (Tyler Hopkins) also trains at Takasago-beya. Other Hawaiians that spent time at Takasago-beya include Koryu (Eric Gaspar) and Nanfu (Kaleo Kekauoha).

Musashigawa-beya

武蔵川部屋

Oyakata:	former yokozuna Mienoumi
Sekitori wrestlers:	Musashimaru (Fiamalu Penitani), Musoyama, Dejima, Wakanoyama, Mutetsuyama
Phone:	03-3802-6333

Wrestlers from Musashi-gawa-beya hosing off after a tough practice.

Musashigawa-beya is one of the most modern stables, with video cameras in the entrance, a complete weight room in the basement, and a spacious *dohyo* and *agarizashiki* (raised viewing area). There is enough room for over fifty guests to watch practice. However, if you want to catch a workout, make sure you go extra early because they usually finish around 10 am (earlier than most stables). If you are visiting during the winter, it may get a little chilly. There are no heaters in the practice area, so bring a coat. Occasionally, they serve hot green tea to help guests keep warm.

CAUTION: The guest bathroom located on the first floor just outside of the viewing area is co-ed. If you are a woman and happen to be using one of the stalls, don't be surprised to see a man doing his business at a urinal.

HOW TO GET THERE: Take the Yamanote Line to Uguisudani Station. After exiting, you can catch a taxi to the stable (about a $7 fare). If you are walking, it will take about 12 minutes.

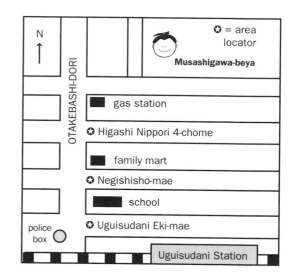

Popular Sumo Stables

安治川部屋

AJIGAWA-BEYA
1-7-4 Mori, Koto-ku, Tokyo 135
Oyakata: ex-yokozuna Asahifuji
Sekitori: none currently
Phone: 03-3634-5514

東関部屋

AZUMAZEKI-BEYA
4-6-4 Higashi-Komagata, Sumida-ku, Tokyo 130

Oyakata: ex-sekiwake Takamiyama
Sekitori: Akebono, Daiki
Phone: 03-3625-0033

出羽海部屋

DEWANOUMI-BEYA
2-3-15 Ryogoku, Sumida-ku, Tokyo 130
Oyakata: ex-sekiwake Washuyama
Sekitori: Kushimaumi, Mainoumi, Ogino-hana, Oginishiki, Dewaarashi
Phone: 03-3632-4920

二子山部屋

FUTAGOYAMA-BEYA

3-10-6 Hon-cho, Nakano-ku, Tokyo 164
Oyakata: ex-ozeki Takanohana
Sekitori: Takanohana, Wakanohana, Taka-nonami, Akinoshima, Takatoriki, Waka-shoyo, Misugisato, Toyonoumi, Gokenzan
Phone: 03-3316-5939

伊勢ノ海部屋

ISENOUMI-BEYA

3-17-6 Harue-cho, Edogawa-ku, Tokyo 132
Oyakata: ex-sekiwake Fujinokawa
Sekitori: Kitakachidoki, Tosanoumi, Oikari
Phone: 03-3677-6860

井筒部屋

IZUTSU-BEYA

2-2-7 Ryogoku, Sumida-ku, Tokyo 130
Oyakata: ex-Sekiwake Sakahoko
Sekitori: Terao, Akinoshu
Phone: 03-3634-9827

春日野部屋

KASUGANO-BEYA

1-7-11 Ryogoku, Sumida-ku, Tokyo 130
Oyakata: ex-Yokozuna Tochinoumi
Sekitori: Tochinowaka, Tochitenko, Tochi-nonada
Phone: 03-3634-9838

北の湖部屋

KITANOUMI-BEYA

2-10-11 Kiyosumi, Koto-ku, Tokyo 135
Oyakata: ex-yokozuna Kitanoumi
Sekitori: Kanechika, Ganyu
Phone: 03-3630-9900

九重部屋

KOKONOE-BEYA

4-22-4 Ishihara, Sumida-ku, Tokyo 130
Oyakata: ex-yokozuna Chiyonofuji
Sekitori: Tomoefuji, Chiyotaikai, Chiyo-nowaka, Chiyotenzan
Phone: 03-3621-0404

間垣部屋

MAGAKI-BEYA

3-8-1 Kamezawa, Sumida-ku, Tokyo 130
Oyakata: ex-yokozuna Wakanohana II
Sekitori: Yamato, Gojoro, Wakanojo
Phone: 03-3626-7449

陸奥部屋

MICHINOKU-BEYA

4-23-18 Horie, Urayasu-shi, Chiba-ken 272
Oyakata: ex-maegashira Hoshiiwato
Sekitori: Hoshiandesu, Hoshitango
Phone: 04-7381-4725

武蔵川部屋

MUSASHIGAWA-BEYA

4-27-1 Nishi-Nippori, Arakawa-ku, Tokyo 116
Oyakata: ex-yokozuna Mienoumi
Sekitori: Musashimaru, Musoyama, De-jima, Mutetsuyama, Wakanoyama
Phone: 03-3802-6333

二所ノ関部屋

NISHONOSEKI-BEYA

4-17-1 Ryogoku, Sumida-ku, Tokyo 130
Oyakata: ex-sekiwake Kongo
Sekitori: Daizen
Phone: 03-3631-0179

大島部屋

OSHIMA-BEYA

3-5-3 Ryogoku, Sumida-ku, Tokyo 130
Oyakata: ex-ozeki Asahikuni
Sekitori: Asahiyutaka, Kyokushuzan, Kyokutenho, Asahisato
Phone: 03-3631-9708

押尾川部屋

OSHIOGAWA-BEYA

2-17-7 Kiba, Koto-ku, Tokyo 135
Oyakata: ex-ozeki Daikirin
Sekitori: Daishi
Phone: 03-3642-4362

121

立浪部屋

TATSUNAMI-BEYA
3-26-2 Ryogoku, Sumida-ku, Tokyo 130
Oyakata: ex-sekiwake Haguroyama
Sekitori: Tomonohana, Daishoho
Phone: 03-3624-4448

時津風部屋

TOKITSUKAZE-BEYA
3-15-3 Ryogoku, Sumida-ku, Tokyo 130
Oyakata: ex-ozeki Yutakayama
Sekitori: Tokisunada, Aogiyama,
Tokitsuumi
Phone: 03-3634-8549

友綱部屋

TOMOZUNA-BEYA
1-20-7 Mori, Koto-ku, Tokyo 135
Oyakata: ex-sekiwake Kaiki
Sekitori: Kaio, Sentoryu
Phone: 03-3631-6390

若松部屋

WAKAMATSU-BEYA
3-5-4 Honjo, Sumida-ku, Tokyo 130
Oyakata: ex-ozeki Asashio
Sekitori: Asanowaka, Asanosho
Phone: 03-5608-3223

佐渡ヶ嶽部屋

SADOGATAKE-BEYA
39 Kushizaki Minami-cho, Matsudo, Chiba 271
Oyakata: ex-yokozuna Kotozakura
Sekitori: Kotonishiki, Kotonowaka, Koto-beppu, Kotoinazuma, Kotoryu, Kotoga-ume, Kotokanyu
Phone: 03-3625-6951

大鵬部屋

TAIHO-BEYA
2-8-3 Kiyosumi, Koto-ku, Tokyo 135
Oyakata: ex-yokozuna Taiho
Sekitori: Dairyu, Ohinode
Phone: 03-3630-4243

高田川部屋

TAKADAGAWA-BEYA
2-1-15 Ichinoe, Edogawa-ku, Tokyo 132
Oyakata: ex-ozeki Maenoyama
Sekitori: Kenko, Zenshinyama
Phone: 03-3656-5604

高砂部屋

TAKASAGO-BEYA
1-16-5 Hashiba, Taito-ku, Tokyo 111
Oyakata: ex-komusubi Fujinishiki
Sekitori: Konishiki, Mitoizumi, Sunahama
Phone: 03-3876-7770

It costs an enormous amount of money to open a stable. Consequently, the Sumo Association supports each oyakata with a salary along with a monthly allowance to help cover operating expenses. An oyakata also receives $600 a month for each wrestler he trains that is ranked below juryo. He is additionally rewarded for developing a sekitori wrestler. Before every tournament, depending on the rank of the sekitori, the stable receives a bonus of:

$300 for every juryo wrestler
$500 for every maegashira wrestler
$1,000 for every sanyaku wrestler
$2,000 for every ozeki wrestler
$3,000 for every yokozuna wrestler

The Hawaiian Wave

Takamiyama

Akebono

Konishiki

Musashimaru

TAKAMIYAMA (Azumazeki)

高見山

Name:	Jesse James Walani Kuhaulua		*Yusho*:	1
	(Watanabe Daigoro)*		**Highest rank:**	sekiwake
Stable:	Takasago		**Best technique:**	*yorikiri*
Birthdate:	6-16-44		**Marital status:**	married
Height/weight:	6'3"/452 lbs.**		**Retired:**	May 1984
Hometown:	Maui, Hawaii		**Elder name:**	Azumazeki
Pro debut:	March 1964		**Oyakata of:**	Azumazeki-beya

* = adopted Japanese name
** = when active

There were a few foreign sumo wrestlers from Asia and Brazil before the 1960s, but none of them found much success in Japan. It can be said that the modern history of foreigners in sumo started with Jesse Kuhaulua. He is known as the Jackie Robinson of sumo: the barrier breaker. Jesse started sumo when he was in high school as a way of training his legs for football. He was working for a pineapple cannery when he decided to go to Japan and try his luck in sumo's home country. When he stepped off the plane, it was the first time in his life he had seen snow. He immediately felt homesick: "The moment that I arrived, I felt blind, deaf, and dumb. I could barely communicate with only a couple of people."

In March 1964, Jesse made his professional debut wrestling under his own name. Soon after, he was given the *shikona* Takamiyama (High Mountain), the fighting name of his stable's founder, Takasago Uragoro. Outside of the ring, Takamiyama struggled to adjust to the new lifestyle that was instantly being forced upon him—the early hours, the rigorous practice schedule, the constant cleaning and cooking chores, being allowed to eat only two meals a day of *chankonabe*, and having to serve at the beck and call of senior wrestlers. He felt like a slave. But worst of all, he felt so alone.

Along with the language barrier, Jesse ran into many cultural barriers. He was heckled in practice for grunting as he did in football and for jumping into the tub soapy without rinsing off first, Japanese style. Some days, he would get on the Yamanote Line and ride the train around and around Tokyo in an endless circle. With his head buried in his hands to hide the tears, he would cry for hours. All he could think about was quitting and going back home to Hawaii.

Although Jesse was struggling, he kept practicing and was determined to give his best. His effort quickly paid off, as he won the jonokuchi division and then two months later the jonidan division as well. In March of 1967, he reached a milestone as the first non-Asian to reach the juryo level. Less than two years later, he reached the top makuuchi division. He stayed at that level for the next sixteen years, during which time he became extremely popular for his good-natured personality.

Takamiyama was truly a tough guy who never gave up. His ironman record for most consecutive tournaments (97) and most consecutive bouts in the makuuchi division (1,398) still stands today. His highest rank was sekiwake, which he achieved after winning the 1972 Nagoya Basho with a 13–2 record, thus reaching another milestone as the first foreigner to win a tournament. President Nixon sent a telegram of congratulations that was read by U.S. Ambassador Ingersoll. It was the only time English has ever been spoken on the *dohyo* during a tournament.

Out of the ring, Jesse took part in an *omiai* (preliminary meeting for an arranged marriage). Although he was nervous about meeting a potential bride, he instantly fell in love when he set eyes on Watanabe Kazue. They were married in February of 1974. Together they had two children, a son, Yumitaro, and later a daughter, Rie.

In 1976, the Sumo Association passed a new rule stating that only Japanese nationals would be able to purchase the stock necessary to become an elder. No explanation was given, but many believe that the aim was to stop foreigners from remaining in sumo after retirement and having an influence on the evolution and organization of the sport. Some thought that a special exception should be made for Takamiyama because of his great success. The association stood its ground and declared that no exceptions would be made.

Jesse was stuck and did not know what to do. He did not want to give up his American citizenship, but he also wanted to remain in the only occupation he had trained in for almost twenty years. The sport had become a part of his life that he did not want to lose. Consequently, in June of 1980, he applied for Japanese citizenship and took the new name Watanabe Daigoro. The personal name comes from his sumo name, and the family name from his wife's name.

Although Jesse wanted to be the first active wrestler in his forties, a series of injuries forced him to retire after the Natsu Basho in 1984. Before a standing-room-only crowd, his topknot was cut off in the traditional style at the Kokugikan in Ryogoku. He was only one month short of his fortieth birthday.

Jesse then took the elder name Azu-

Azumazeki Oyakata (right) with his prize pupil Akebono at Akebono's yokozuna acceptance ceremony.

mazeki and coached for a short time at Takasago-beya. In April of 1986 he broke off and started his own stable from scratch, taking with him no sponsors or wrestlers. The odds were against him. "It was hard at first because I started with nothing. A lot of people said I couldn't do it. But sumo is my life, and after I retired I wanted to pass on my knowledge." Initially he had only Japanese wrestlers, but he later added foreigners.

Jesse firmly explains that his Azumazeki stable is no different from other stables run by Japanese oyakata. He is very strict and demanding with his wrestlers. "I want my wrestlers to practice more. To give 100 percent is not enough. You have to give more than 150 percent. You have to do more than everyone else to succeed."

Jesse's preaching has quickly paid off. Only four years later, in 1990, his star pupil, Akebono, reached juryo and became his first sekitori. Akebono has gone on to surpass all expectations and has become the first foreign yokozuna. As of 1997, there is one other Hawaiian in the stable: Daiki (Percy Kitapa) in the juryo division.

Now that Azumazeki has reached his goal of training a grand champion, he has only two goals remaining. "The first is to make a Japanese sekitori. I don't have anyone close yet, but I'm still trying. The second is what everyone, including my own kids, keep bugging me about . . . to lose some weight!"

KONISHIKI

小錦

Name:	Salevaa Atisanoe
	(Shioda Yasokichi)*
Stable:	Takasago
Birthdate:	12-31-63
Height/weight:	6'0"/604 lbs.
Hometown:	Nanakuli, Hawaii
Pro debut:	July 1982
Yusho:	3

Highest rank:	ozeki
Best technique:	*oshidashi, yorikiri*
Marital status:	married
Favorite food:	"anything"
Hobby:	piano, surfing the Internet
Nickname:	Sale (sa-lei)

* = adopted Japanese name

Salevaa Atisanoe graduated near the top of his University High School class in Honolulu, Hawaii. He was a star football player and planned on going off to law school. Then he met Jesse Kuhaulua (Takamiyama). Jesse convinced him to try sumo, a sport in which his big body would be advantageous. Atisanoe was hesitant; as he put it, "I don't like to fight." But it was an interesting opportunity, and he knew that his family, with nine children, was struggling. After arriving in Japan, he was astonished when he saw the sumo "uniform" consisting of one *mawashi* and nothing else. "I was so ashamed wearing a G-string," he explained. But worse were the intense workouts that left him exhausted, and the endless daily chores. As he explained it, "When I first got here, I was abused every day. It reached the point where I just got used to pain."

The senior wrestlers who tormented him were the same ones that he would later have to serve without complaint; scrubbing them in the bath, serving their meals, taking telephone calls, and running their errands. "When you are at the bottom, you have to take everything. You have to get used to being stepped on. I had it really bad." He decided he would have to move up in the ranks quickly so that he could get out of the servant work. He improved his pushing technique and, with his weight advantage, he started to overpower his opponents. Because he showed promise, he was given the fighting name

Konishiki Yasokichi, after the stable's yokozuna of the 1890s. Living up to the name, he won the jonokuchi and jonidan divisions with perfect records of 7–0. After only one year, he reached the juryo level and became a sekitori.

Konishiki describes his own fighting as "strictly offensive." He does not use counter techniques but simply tries to power his opponent out of the ring using his massive girth. This strategy was successful. After winning his first tournament in 1989, Konishiki was very emotional and cried tears of joy. He had become only the second foreigner (after Takamiyama) to win a tournament.

Many fans were curious about what the 600-pound American did out of the ring. There were stories about him dancing the entire night away at local discos, about him drinking over a hundred bottles of beer in one sitting. Yet many also admired him for his persistence and honesty. He worked hard in the ring and always expressed his views frankly. The Japanese, in their rigid society, never

Laughing it up—Konishiki style!

really have the chance to publicly express their true feelings.

Konishiki was sometimes thought to be a little too blunt, but many envied his frankness. He has an easygoing personality, has studied and become fluent in the Japanese language, plays the piano and golf, and has an awesome singing voice that he loves to show-off at karaoke contests on television. He is personable, extra huggable, knowledgeable on practically every subject, and has the biggest cannonball dive on the planet.

But around 1984, there emerged an anti-Konishiki faction. Conservatives opposed not only Konishiki, but the idea of having any foreigners in the national sport. They did not like to see foreigners quickly gaining rank and then have to watch their own Japanese wrestlers walk behind them. Since Konishiki was the highest ranked of all foreigners at the time, much of the resentment was directed at him. The conservatives never really understood him and complained he was too "un-Japanese" and lacked humility and respect, the all-important quality of *hinkaku*. "It was really bad," Konishiki remembers. "I had a hard time falling asleep at night. All of the bad things that they were saying about me really hurt. It took me about a year to get over it and just say, 'What the heck! I gotta do what I gotta do!'" Konishiki went on to reach ozeki rank (which he held for thirty-nine consecutive tournaments) and has won a total of three tournaments to date. Although he fell short of the exalted yokozuna rank, he had become a dominant force in the world of sumo.

On February 11, 1992, Konishiki married former fashion model Shioda Sumika. After saying their vows in a Christian church ceremony, which was broadcast

Konishiki arriving at the arena for another tournament.

live on Japanese prime time television, he kissed her forehead explaining, "Well, I didn't want to mess up her make-up." The following reception was attended by 1,500 guests.

On February 1, 1994, Konishiki was granted Japanese citizenship from the Japanese Justice Ministry. He officially changed his name to Shioda Yasokichi (the family name coming from his wife and the personal name from his sumo name). He has already purchased the necessary elder stock that allows him to become an oyakata and take the name Sanoyama after retiring.

A series of knee injuries has forced Konishiki to drop from the ozeki rank. But he plans to continue wrestling. "Of course I want to stay in the top division, but I'm going to continue wrestling until I can't walk. I know that most Japanese wrestlers would quit right away, not to lose face, but I like sumo. I want to continue. Can you believe that when I take a bath, guys wipe my back. . . . even my feet?! Do you know of any baseball or basketball player that gets his feet wiped? Sumo is my life and once you retire, you can never go back."

In February 1997 Konishiki invited thirty-five needy schoolchildren from Hawaii to Tokyo to see a tournament, go to Disneyland, and hang out with some other Hawaiian rikishi. "I wanted to give something back to the kids of Hawaii. When I was little I never realized it's such a big world out there. I wanted the kids to know your background doesn't matter, as long as you keep dreaming."

Konishiki is truly a man with a heart bigger than his body. For now, he keeps on fighting "the war," as he calls it. If this fun-loving man doesn't become a coach one day, his secret ambition is to become the ambassador to Japan. With multi-talented, Konishiki, *anything* is possible!

AKEBONO

曙

Name:	Chad George Haaheo Rowan (Akebono Taro)*	**Highest rank:**	yokozuna
		Best technique:	*tsukidashi, yorikiri*
Stable:	Azumazeki	**Marital status:**	single
Birthdate:	5-8-69	**Favorite food:**	Mom's meatloaf
Height/weight:	6'8"/484 lbs.	**Hobby:**	listening to music
Hometown:	Waimanalo, Hawaii	**Nickname:**	(none)
Pro debut:	March 1988		
Yusho:	8 (to date)		

* = adopted Japanese name

Akebono, who is of Hawaiian, Irish, and Cuban descent, was born on May 8, 1969, and grew up in Waimanalo. He liked sports and participated in local baseball and basketball leagues. He played basketball at Kaiser High School and later at Hawaii Pacific University on a scholarship. As he explains, "I wasn't really going to college for school. I was missing classes, but still making passing grades. I could have gotten a degree, but it wouldn't have meant anything. I was mainly going to play basketball." Less than a year after he began, personal differences with the coach forced him to leave the program. A family friend then introduced him to Azumazeki Oyakata (formerly Jesse Kuhaulua, or Takamiyama). Chad was interested in trying sumo, but Azumazeki thought that the eighteen year old at 6'5" and 310 pounds was too tall to become a wrestler. A low center of gravity is the

Akebono showing off a gold ring he was given upon his promotion to yokozuna.

key to balance, so Azumazeki wanted to take Chad's younger and shorter brother, George, who at 6'1" and 260 pounds had the ideal sumo body. But George was still in high school, so Chad, who promised to work hard and never give up, was finally accepted. Carrying only one suitcase, he left for a new life in Japan in 1988.

Rowan made his debut in March of 1988 under the name of Daikai (Great Sea). Adjustment to the grueling sumo lifestyle was difficult. For the first six months, he called his mother every day and cried himself to sleep. "I thought that I was a man, but I was only a baby. I had to throw out everything I had learned in my first eighteen years in Hawaii and start over. Even though I wanted to quit, I couldn't. If I did, everyone would tease my parents and say, 'How come you have a boy so big that can't do anything?' I had to show everyone that I could do it." On top of it all, the strict ranking system was probably the hardest for him to comprehend. "I couldn't understand why fifteen- and sixteen-year-old kids were ordering me around to get them things and to do chores like cleaning the toilets. Just because they joined the stable before me, they had the 'right' to as my *senpai* or senior."

Rowan's fighting name was changed to Akebono and he quickly moved up the ranks. In March of 1990, he reached the juryo division and became Azumazeki's first sekitori. A little over two years later

Akebono performing the yokozuna dohyo-iri.

he won his first championship with a record of 13–2. After his promotion to ozeki, he became stronger and stronger. His powerful fighting style started to dominate. In most of his matches his opponents had absolutely no chance as he pushed and slammed them out of the ring within a couple of seconds. In November of 1992 and then in January of 1993, Akebono won back-to-back tournaments and became the first foreigner to be promoted to sumo's highest rank of yokozuna. Perhaps even more amazing is that the American became yokozuna in the shortest amount of time in the sport's history.

On January 27, 1993, Akebono officially became the sports sixty-fourth grand champion. Speaking softly in polite Japanese he replied, "I humbly accept, and will devote myself in practice and promise not to defile the status of grand champion." The following day, a three-hour ceremony was held at Meiji Shrine in western Tokyo, where he was presented with his first *tsuna* (belt) to be worn during the yokozuna's *dohyo-iri* (ring-entering ceremony). In front of an audience of 4,000 fans and well wishers, Akebono endured snow flurries and performed his first *dohyo-iri*.

Since his promotion, Akebono has lived like a fish in a fishbowl with everyone watching him. For the amount of pressure and responsibility that he has, he handles it well—in his own laid-back style Whether he wins or loses, he is respectful to reporters and answers their questions.

He plays with children and rarely refuses an autograph. He helps train lower-ranked wrestlers and often takes them out at his own expense. Akebono only regrets not being able to return home more often (he keeps up with everything in America, though, through cable TV, videos, and CDs).

Unfortunately, Akebono's 474-pound frame has taken a beating over these past few years. In June of 1994, Akebono had operations on both of his knees. Although the operations were successful, he was ordered by his doctors to lose weight. His massive upper body was putting too much stress on his knees. Akebono began an intense rehabilitation and diet program. He sat out two consecutive tournaments but came back to win the *yusho* in the March 1995 tournament.

Yet Akebono's constant injuries have made winning difficult recently. He wonders how much longer he will be able to compete in the sport he has grown to love. He wants to try to "get back on track" and regain his winning ways. Life at the top, as a yokozuna, is hard. If you don't win, you are almost forced to retire so as not to disgrace the title.

But don't count Akebono out. The big wrestler says that he still has a little left in his gas tank to try for a few more championships. Regardless of the result, as the first foreign yokozuna, Chad Rowan has made history in the sport of sumo.

"The glare"—Akebono's intensity before a bout is well known.

MUSASHIMARU

武蔵丸

Name:	Fiamalu Penitani (Musashimaru Koyo)*	**Highest rank:**	ozeki
		Best technique:	*yorikiri, oshidashi*
Stable:	Musashigawa	**Marital status:**	single
Birthdate:	5-2-71	**Favorite food:**	Hawaiian plate lunches
Height/weight:	6'3"/447 lbs.	**Hobby:**	listening to reggae music
Hometown:	Waianae, Hawaii	**Nickname:**	Maru
Pro debut:	September 1989		
Yusho:	2		

* = adopted Japanese name

Fiamalu Penitani was born in Samoa and lived there his first ten years. His parents then relocated the family (five boys and three girls) to Hawaii. Fiamalu, the fourth son, was very athletic and excelled in sports. At Waianae High School he was a defensive lineman on the football team as well as a member of the Greco-Roman wrestling team. During his senior year he was offered football scholarships to several junior colleges, but turned them all down. "I was never really into school," he says.

One day, while wrestling in a meet, he was spotted by Date Jiichiro, a gold medal winner in wrestling at the Montreal Olympics. Date introduced him to Musashigawa Oyakata, who thought that the muscular youth might have sumo potential. But he was hesitant to accept a foreigner. A year earlier he had taken in another American, William Molina (Musashinobo). Things had not worked out for Molina, and he had quickly returned home. Adjustment to sumo life can be difficult even for a Japanese, and it is almost always harder for a *gaijin*. In the end, Musashigawa Oyakata decided to accept Penitani in the stable, but only for a few months on a trial basis. In the summer of 1989, Penitani informally entered the *heya*. If at the end of the trial period he thought he could handle the sumo lifestyle, he would be allowed to officially join the stable. If not, he was free to return home.

The adjustment to life in Japan was difficult for Penitani. He wasn't particular-

ly fond of Japanese food, and he struggled with the language barrier. For the entire first month, he did not call home even once. He explained that he was so homesick that if he called, he would probably break down and want to return to Hawaii. In spite of his hardships, he was doing well in practice and could see a future for himself in sumo. Musashigawa Oyakata was also pleased with his new recruit. Penitani showed more potential than he had originally thought. Soon after, he officially joined the stable and was given the *shikona* Musashimaru. *Musashi* came from the stable's name and *maru* was the Japanese pronunciation of part of his own name (Fiamalu). The suffix *-maru* is also commonly affixed to the names of ships in Japan, and since Fia was from Hawaii it appeared to fit him well.

Musashimaru made his debut in November 1989. He

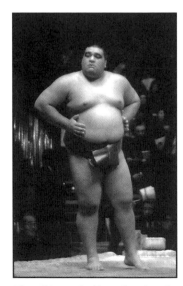

Musashimaru looking relaxed on the dohyo.

won the *yusho* in the jonokuchi division, followed by the *yusho* in the sandanme division the next year. By July of 1991 he had been promoted to juryo and thus become Musashigawa's first sekitori. "Although I'm going solo [being the only foreigner in the stable], from that time on, I've been the king over here." He won the title in his first juryo tournament and set the record as the first foreigner to win the division. Although most young wrestlers have to go through years of harsh servant duty, Musashimaru's rise in the rankings was so fast that he got out of it very quickly. "When I first came over, I had to do the cleaning like everybody else. Sometimes they let me off a little easier because I couldn't really understand the language. But then I rose in the ranks real fast, and before I knew it, I had people working under me."

Since his debut in the makuuchi division, Musashimaru has never once had a losing record in a tournament. In January of 1994 he was promoted to ozeki. Only six months later, at the Nagoya Basho, he went undefeated and claimed his first championship, the first foreigner to win a tournament with a perfect 15–0 record. He won his second championship in 1996 in a historic five-man play-off.

As Musashimaru goes up in the ranks, he is also going up in the popularity polls. He is still learning Japanese but is well liked by his fellow wrestlers for his easy-going, playful personality. His ideal sumo body and cute cartoon-character-like face, which many Japanese believe resembles that of their historic hero of the 1870s, Saigo Takamori, gives his many admirers all the more reason to feel a close connection with him. Musashimaru, who is Samoan, Tongan, German, and Portuguese, explains, "I'm always being told how I look so Japanese. But can you believe it? Look at me. Don't I look like I'm from Hawaii?"

Many say Musashimaru is almost a perfect ozeki. He is rarely injured, just about always gets at least ten wins, and is a likeable personality. In his free time Musashimaru used to enjoy going out, especially to the discos in Roppongi or "listening" to others sing karaoke (he doesn't like singing himself). But with the many strict rules of living in a stable, mainly curfew, his love of nightlife created a problem for him. "You know, when I go out, I like to go out." Going out usually meant coming home late, and Musashigawa-beya, one of the most modern sumo stables, has video cameras posted all around the entrances. A wrestler out past curfew will get caught. To avoid this, Musashimaru would sometimes stay out all night, returning just before practice the next morning—a remarkable feat considering how strenuous the practice workouts can be.

These days, with or without the curfew, Musashimaru now actually prefers staying home. He has become such a recognized star that "it's really become too much of a hassle for me to go out anymore. It becomes uncomfortable, not only for myself, but for everyone else involved. I always have to stop and take pictures or sign autographs. One time I went into a record store and by the time I got my CD, we couldn't get out. Even when my brother comes to visit, I can't take him around. I have to send one of the younger boys [his tsukebito, or attendant] to take him."

So, for now, Musashimaru regularly works out with weights at the stable's gym in the basement to the blasting sound of reggae music. Although he misses Hawaiian plate lunches, American television, and playing football, he realizes that, as an ozeki, "my life is here in Japan, in sumo. I don't want to go back yet."

A local Hawaiian guy all the way: Musashimaru.

OTHER FOREIGN RIKISHI

ACTIVE FOREIGN WRESTLERS

Kyokushuzan

Name:	Daver Batbayal
Stable:	Oshima
Birthdate:	3-8-73
Height/weight:	5'11½"/271 lbs.
Hometown:	Mongolia
Pro debut:	March 1992
Highest rank:	komusubi

One of the smaller rikishi in the top division, Kyoskushuzan is a skilled technician with great fighting spirit who employs a variety of techniques for his wins. He came to Japan with five other Mongolians and is the highest ranked of the three who remain.

Yamato

Name:	George Kalima
Stable:	Magaki
Birthdate:	12-17-69
Height/weight:	6'1"/419 lbs.
Hometown:	Oahu, Hawaii
Pro debut:	November 1990
Highest rank:	maegashira 12

Yamato uses his solid pushing techniques to bulldoze opponents out of the ring. He concentrates on his "own sumo style" rather than on what his opponent is thinking. His younger brother (both are from Akebono's hometown) did sumo but has since returned to Hawaii.

Sunahama

Name:	Tyler Hopkins
Stable:	Takasago
Birthdate:	7-21-71
Height/weight:	5'9"/422 lbs.
Hometown:	Oahu, Hawaii
Pro debut:	September 1990
Highest rank:	juryo 5

Sunahama has a powerful tachiai—one of the strongest in the entire juryo division. Although an intense fighter in the ring, he is friendly and easygoing. He came to Japan with two other Hawaiians (Nanfu and Koryu), but is now the only one who remains.

Sentoryu

Name:	Henry Miller
Stable:	Tomozuna
Birthdate:	7-16-69
Height/weight:	5'7"/283 lbs.
Hometown:	St. Louis, Missouri
Pro debut:	July 1988
Highest rank:	juryo 9

Muscular Sentoryu should be in the makuuchi division, but injuries have kept him fighting between the makushita and juryo divisions. He was a star football player and wrestler in high school, and he is the only rikishi who is half Black and half Japanese.

Daiki

Name:	Percy Kitapa
Stable:	Azumazeki
Birthdate:	7-16-73
Height/weight:	6'1"/468 lbs.
Hometown:	Oahu, Hawaii
Pro debut:	November 1991
Highest rank:	juryo 10

Daiki is the second sekitori for Azumazeki-beya (the first is Akebono). A good fighter on the belt, Daiki can usually win when he gets a good hold of his opponent's mawashi with his right hand. He spends his time weight training as he battles between makushita and juryo.

RETIRED AMERICAN RIKISHI

Nanfu
Name:	Kaleo Kekauoha
Stable:	Takasago
Birthdate:	1-22-70
Height/weight:	5'8"/275 lbs.
Hometown:	Oahu, Hawaii
Pro debut:	September 1990
Highest rank:	makushita 1

Koryu
Name:	Eric Gaspar
Stable:	Takasago
Birthdate:	1-3-70
Height/weight:	6'0"/304 lbs.
Hometown:	Oahu, Hawaii
Pro debut:	September 1990
Highest rank:	makushita 49

Takamio
Name:	John Feleunga
Stable:	Azumazeki
Birthdate:	7-1-67
Height/weight:	6'2"/411 lbs.
Hometown:	Oahu, Hawaii
Pro debut:	July 1986
Highest rank:	makushita 2

Ozora
Name:	Troy Talaimatai
Stable:	Azumazeki
Birthdate:	12-2-71
Height/weight:	6'0"/396 lbs.
Hometown:	Oahu, Hawaii
Pro debut:	September 1988
Highest rank:	makushita 13

Wakachikara
Name:	Glen Kalima
Stable:	Magaki
Birthdate:	12-18-70
Height/weight:	6'1"/278 lbs.
Hometown:	Oahu, Hawaii
Pro debut:	March 1991
Highest rank:	makushita 26

Total Number of Foreigners Who Have Entered Sumo

America	29
Argentina	2
Brazil	11
Canada	1
China	5
England	2
Korea	6
Mongolia	6
Paraguay	1
Philippines	3
Sri Lanka	1
Taiwan	12
Tonga	6
West Samoa	2

Note: Over the years, only nine foreigners have reached the top makuuchi division: Toyonishiki (Colorado), Rikidozan (Korea), Takamiyama (Hawaii), Konishiki (Hawaii), Nankairyu (Samoa), Akebono (Hawaii), Musashimaru (Hawaii), Kyokushuzan (Mongolia), and Yamato (Hawaii).

Autograph of Azumazeki Oyakata (ex-seki-wake Takamiyama), the "father" of foreign participation in sumo.

TEGATA: HAND PRINTS

Tegata are autographed hand prints made by sumotori as souvenirs for their fans, friends, and boosters.

Takanohana.

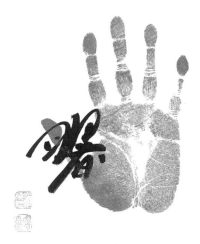

Akebono.

Musashimaru.

Takanonami.

Kaio.

Musoyama.

Konishiki.

Mitoizumi.

Terao.

Tosanoumi.

Mainoumi.

SUMO RECORDS

MOST TOURNAMENT CHAMPIONSHIPS

Taiho	32
Chiyonofuji	31
Kitanoumi	24
Takanohana II	16*
Wajima	14
Futabayama	12
Tsunenohana	10
Tochinishiki	10
Wakanohana I	10
Kitanofuji	10

MOST CONSECUTIVE CHAMPIONSHIPS

Taiho	6
Chiyonofuji	5
Kitanoumi	5
Futabayama	5
Takanohana II	4*

MOST WINS IN MAKUUCHI DIVISION

Chiyonofuji	807
Kitanoumi	804
Taiho	746
Takamiyama	683
Konishiki	628*
Wajima	620
Kashiwado	599
Kitanofuji	592

MOST WINS IN ONE YEAR

Kitanoumi	82
Taiho	81
Chiyonofuji	80
Takanohana II	80*

*still active

MOST CONSECUTIVE WINS IN MAKUUCHI

Futabayama	69
Chiyonofuji	53
Taiho	45
Haguroyama	32
Kitanoumi	32
Takanohana II	30*
Sadanoyama	25
Tochinishiki	24
Wakanohana I	24

The above records are for modern times. During the 1700s, Tanikaze had 63 wins in a row and Raiden had 44. During the 1800s, Umegatani had 58 wins in a row. In the early 1900s, Tachiyama had 56 in a row.

YOUNGEST YOKOZUNA

Kitanoumi	21 years, 2 months
Taiho	22 years, 3 months
Takanohana II	22 years, 6 months
Kashiwado	22 years, 11 months

MOST KINBOSHI

Akinoshima	15*
Takamiyama	12
Annenyama	10
Dewanishiki	10
Kitanonada	10
Ozutsu	10

MOST APPEARANCES IN MAKUUCHI

Takamiyama	1,430
Kirinji	1,221
Tsurugamine	1,128

MOST CONSECUTIVE APPEARANCES IN MAKUUCHI

Takamiyama	1,231
Ozutsu	1,170
Kurohimeyama	1,065

HONBASHO LOCATIONS

HATSU BASHO (JANUARY)
NATSU BASHO (MAY)
AKI BASHO (SEPTEMBER)

Kokugikan
1-3-28 Yokoami, Sumida-ku
Tokyo 130
Phone: 03-3623-5111

HARU BASHO (MARCH)

Osaka Furitsu Taiikukan
(Osaka Prefectural Gymnasium)
3-4-36 Nanbanaka, Naniwa-ku
Osaka 556
Phone: 06-631-0120

NAGOYA BASHO (JULY)
Aichi Kenritsu Taiikukan
(Aichi Prefectural Gymnasium)
1-1 Ninomaru, Naka-ku
Nagoya 460
Phone: 052-971-0015

KYUSHU BASHO (NOVEMBER)

Fukuoka Kokusai Center
(Fukuoka International Center)
2-2 Chikko Honmachi, Hakata-ku
Fukuoka 812
Phone: 092-291-9311

The word *yume*, "dream," as
written and signed by the great
former yokozuna Taiho.

SUMO WORDS

agari zashiki: the elevated area where coaches and visitors sit when viewing practice

akeni: personal bamboo trunks for sekitori wrestlers

ani-deshi: senior wrestler

banzuke: ranking sheet

basho: tournament

bintsuke: wax made of a soybean derivative; used when making a wrestler's topknot

butsukari-geiko: drill where an attacker runs into a defender and pushes him to the edge of the *dohyo*

 *chankonabe*: high-calorie but nutritious daily stew that wrestlers eat; it contains many vegetables, tofu, and meat, chicken, or fish

chaya: tea houses located on the north side of the stadium; box seats may be purchased from a tea house

chikara gami: "power paper" used by sekitori wrestlers for wiping off during pre-bout rituals

chikara mizu: "power water" used by sekitori wrestlers for purification during pre-bout rituals

chonmage: topknot

danpatsu-shiki: retirement ceremony

degeiko: going out to practice at another stable

deshi: an apprentice wrestler (not yet a sekitori)

dohyo-iri: ring-entering ceremony performed separately by the juryo, makuuchi, and yokozuna wrestlers

dohyo: the sumo ring

dohyo matsuri: Shinto ceremony to bless the *dohyo*

eboshi: black hat worn by gyoji

fusa: tassels hanging down from the roof above the *dohyo*

fusen: default

gaijin: a foreigner

geta: Japanese wooden sandals

Ginosho: Technique Award

gohei: A Shinto symbol (a wooden stick with folded white paper attached to it) placed in the *dohyo* after practice is over

"*Gottsuan*": sumo slang for "thank you"

gunbai: referee's war paddle, which he uses to direct wrestlers before and during matches and to signal the winner of a bout

 gunbai-dori: term used if the judges affirm the referee's decision after a *mono-ii* (conference)

gyoji: referee

gyoji matta: referee time out

"*Hakkeyoi*": a gyoji's command meaning "Do something" or "Get going"

hanamichi: "flower paths"; the aisles that the wrestlers use when walking from the dressing rooms to the *dohyo*

hanazumo: non-tournament sumo and sumo-related events

hanko: stamp or seal used for formally certifying documents, similar to a signature in the West; all stables have their own *hanko* and sometimes use it to stamp their high-ranked wrestlers' *tegata*

haori/hakama: Japanese formal wear (coat/pleated pants, almost like a skirt)

hatakikomi: "pull down" technique

heya (-beya): sumo stable

heyagashira: highest-ranking wrestler in a stable

higashi: East (grouping of wrestlers)

hikkake: "pulling" technique

hitatare: gyoji's salary and costume (dependent on rank)

honbasho: tournament

ichidai toshiyori: "one-generation elder" (The honor is given to strong yokozuna so that they can keep their fighting name as an elder name. However, their stock dies with them and cannot be passed down to an apprentice. Currently there are two one-generation elders: Taiho and Kitanoumi.)

ichimon: a group of affiliated stables; the five *ichimon* are Dewanoumi, Nishonoseki, Takasago, Tokitsukaze, and Tatsunami/Isegahama

intai: to retire

"*Jikan desu*" or "*Jikan ippai*": "Time is up" (a gyoji command during matches)

jonidan: second lowest division of wrestlers

jonokuchi: lowest division of wrestlers

jungyo: sumo exhibition tour

juryo: second highest division of wrestlers

kachikoshi: a winning record; for the juryo and makuuchi division, 8 -7 or better, for divisions below juryo, 4-3 or better

kadoban ozeki: an ozeki that had a losing record the previous tournament; if he has another losing record in the following tournament, he will be demoted

kanji[1]: Chinese characters (all sumo names are written with *kanji*)

kanji[2]: supervisor

kanjin-zumo: benefit sumo performed for charity (17th century)

Kantosho: Fighting Spirit Award

keiko: practice

keikoba: the practice area

kensho-kin: envelopes containing "encouragement money" that a winner of a bout receives as a bonus

kesho-mawashi: the fancy ceremonial aprons that sekitori wear for their *dohyo-iri*

kettei-sen: a playoff

ki: heart, spirit, mind, as in *Ki ga haitte imasu* (He is really psyched)

kimarite: winning technique

Kimura Shonosuke: the name always given to the top referee

kinboshi: "gold star"; given to a maegashira wrestler who defeats a yokozuna

kinjite: foul or illegal technique

kodomo-zumo: children's sumo

koenkai: organization that sponsors a stable or an individual wrestler

kohai: a junior (younger or lower in rank)

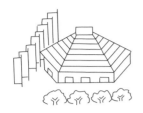

Kokugikan: sumo arena in Ryogoku, Tokyo

komusubi: fourth highest rank in the top makuuchi division

Kosho Seido: Public Injury System that allows an injured wrestler to sit out a tournament without affecting his rank

kubinage: "headlock throw" technique

kuroboshi: "black star"; a loss

maegashira: fifth highest rank in the makuuchi division (divided into East and West, the wrestlers are ranked 1 to 12, 13, or 14 depending on the number of wrestlers at the time)

maezumo: "pre-sumo" division; after graduating from this level a wrestler's name will appear on the ranking sheet

makekoshi: a losing record; for juryo and makuuchi division, 7–8 or worse; for divisions below juryo, 3–4 or worse

makushita: third highest division (just below juryo)

makushita tsukedashi: an exemption for college champions that allows them to enter the sumo rankings at the bottom of makushita (instead of at *maezumo*)

makuuchi: top division above juryo

man-in onrei: "Full house, thank you"; the banners that hang above the *dohyo* during sold-out tournaments

masu-zeki: box seats on the first floor of the arena that seat four people

matawari: sumo-style splits

matta: "wait"; sumo wrestler who makes a false start or is not ready when time has expired (juryo wrestlers are fined $500 and makuuchi wrestlers $1,000 for committing *matta*)

mawashi: sumo wrestler's belt

mizuhiki-maku: purple curtain that hangs down from the *yakata* or roof

mochi-kyukin: incentive pay for wrestlers ranked in the juryo division or above, based on the number of points a wrestler has accumulated

mono-ii: conference by the judges to decide on a close match

morozashi: during a fight, the situation of a wrestler having both hands on his opponent's belt

musubi no ichiban: the last match of the day

myoseki: the 105 elder names

nagezawa: throwing techniques

nakabi: middle day of a tournament

nekodamashi: when a wrestler claps his hands together in front of his opponent's face (during the *tachiai*) and then immediately darts to the side or underneath to try to get a good position (smaller wrestlers, like Mainoumi, sometimes use this technique to momentarily distract their opponent)

NHK: Japan Broadcasting Corporation; the semi-governmental station that broadcasts the sumo tournaments live in Japan

Nihon Sumo Kyokai: Japan Sumo Association

niramiai: staring contest between wrestlers that takes place at the center of the ring before a bout

nishi: West (grouping of wrestlers)

nobori: colorful banners with the wrestlers' names and stable names posted outside the sumo arena during a tournament

"*Nokotta*": gyoji's command meaning "You're still in"

obi: belt or sash worn around the waist over a kimono

ofuro: bath

oichomage: fancy topknot, resembling a ginkgo leaf, worn by sekitori wrestlers

okamisan: stablemaster's wife

oshi: pushing

oshidashi: "push out" technique

osumo-san: a sumo wrestler

oyakata: stablemaster or coach

ozeki: second highest rank in the top makuuchi division

rensho: consecutive wins

riji: director (of the Sumo Association)

rijicho: chairman (of the Sumo Association)

rikishi: "strong man"; that is, a sumo wrestler

sagari: decorative strings that hang down from the *mawashi*; they are only worn during tournaments

sanban-geiko: series of practice matches against one opponent

sandanme: third lowest division

sansho: the three special awards (Technique, Fighting Spirit, and Outstanding Performance); each is worth $20,000

sanyaku: collective term for the sekiwake and komusubi ranks

sashichigai: judges' overruling of a referee's decision

sekitori: sumo wrestler in the juryo or makuuchi division

sekiwake: third highest rank in the top makuuchi division

senpai: a senior (older or higher in rank)

senshuraku: last day of a tournament

setta: Japanese-style tatami slippers

sewanin: position in the Sumo Association for retired wrestlers as operations assistants; affiliated with a stable and help with stable operations as well

Shikimori Inosuke: name always given to the second-ranked referee

shikiri: pre-bout warm up

shikiri-sen: the two starting lines where the *tachiai* takes place in the center of the ring

shikishi: customary paper used for autographs in Japan; it is square, hard (like cardboard), and usually white with gold trim

shiko: foot stomping used for warm up in training and rituals

shikona: fighting name

shindeshi: a new recruit

shindeshi kensa: examination for new recruits

shinitai: "dead body"; a wrestler in a losing position that he cannot recover from

shinpan: five ringside judges (all former wrestlers) with the power to overrule a gyoji's decision

Shinto: Japan's indigenous animist religion

shio: salt, thrown by a wrestler to purify the ring before a match *shiranui* style: one of two styles for a yokozuna's belt and *dohyo-iri*; named after Shiranui Koemon of the late Edo period

shiroboshi: "white star"; a win

shisho: head coach, or oyakata, who owns the stable

shitakubeya: sumo wrestlers' locker or dressing room

shitatedashinage: "underarm throw-out" technique

shitatenage: "underarm throw" technique

shobu shinpan: judges who sit at ringside during a bout

shokkiri: comic sumo often performed at exhibitions

shomen: main side of the arena

shonichi: opening day of a tournament

Shukunsho: Outstanding Performance Award (usually based on the number of upsets over ozeki and yokozuna)

shusse hiro: ceremony introducing new recruits, usually held on the eighth day of a tournament

sonkyo: breathing deeply in an almost meditative state, usually done at the end of practice

soppu (chankonabe): basic *chanko* style in which a chicken bone is boiled to make a broth

sotogake: "outside leg trip" technique

sukuinage: "beltless arm throw" technique

sumo jinku: sumo songs written by yobidashi; a group of wrestlers will often perform them at exhibitions

sumo moji: stylized "sumo" calligraphy used on the *banzuke* (ranking sheet)

sumotori: a sumo wrestler

sunakaburi: "sand covered"; the first six rows of seats at sumo arenas

suriashi: leg strengthener done in a crouched position with the hands in front, bent at the elbows; the wrestler steps forward alternating legs, or jumps together with both legs, pushing with the arms and keeping his body low to the ground

tabi: Japanese-style toed socks

tachiai: initial clash when the wrestlers charge at each other in the ring

tachimochi: swordbearer for the yokozuna *dohyo-iri*

taisho: small sword carried by the tate-gyoji in his *obi*

tanimachi: sumo patrons

tate gyoji: the two top-ranking referees

tawara: rice-straw bundles that make the borders around the *dohyo*

tegata: autographed hand prints made by sekitori wrestlers

Tenno-hai: Emperor's Cup (the championship trophy)

tenran-zumo: sumo that takes place in the presence of the emperor or crown prince

teppo: long wooden pole in the corner of the practice area, used to strengthen the arms and for improving pushing techniques

teuchi-shiki: ceremony held after the awards ceremony on the last day of a tournament to welcome the new recruits who have just finished their first tournament

tojitsu-ken: daily tickets that cannot be purchased in advance but only in the morning on the day of the match (must be used the same day)

tokei-gakari: shinpan who is the timekeeper

tokoyama: sumo hairdresser

tokudawara: four bales on the ring that protrude slightly out of the circle; when sumo was held outdoors, the space was used to drain water

tomonokai: "friendship clubs" made up of boosters who support a stable

torikumi: a sumo bout

torinaoshi: redo of a match because there was no clear winner (decided by the judges after calling a *mono-ii*)

toshiyori: elder

toshiyori kabu: the elder stock necessary for becoming an oyakata

tsukebito: apprentice assigned to take care of a sekitori wrestler

tsuki: slapping or thrusting

tsukioshi: pushing and shoving techniques

tsuna: yokozuna's ceremonial belt

tsunauchi-shiki: ceremony for making the yokozuna's belt

tsuppari: slapping

tsuridashi: "carry out" technique

tsuritaoshi: "carry down" technique

tsuyu-harai: "dew sweeper" for the yokozuna *dohyo-iri*

uchiage: party held after completion of a basho

uchigake: "inside leg trip" technique

unryu style: one of the two styles for a yokozuna's belt and *dohyo-iri*; it is named after Unryu Hisayoshi of the late Edo period

uwatedashinage: "overarm throw-out" technique

uwatenage: "over-arm throw" technique

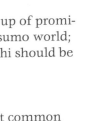

wakaimono-gashira: position for wrestlers in the Sumo Association after retirement; responsible for keeping records and helping out at tournaments and exhibitions

yaguradaiko: *taiko* drum in the 52-foot tower outside the arena, played to signal the end of the tournament day

yakuza: gangster

yaocho: fixed match

yobidashi: ring attendant

yokozuna: highest rank; a yokozuna can never be demoted

Yokozuna Shingi-iinkai: Yokozuna Deliberation Council, made up of prominent men from outside the sumo world; the council decides if a rikishi should be promoted to yokozuna

yori: grappling or clinching

yorikiri: "force out"; the most common winning technique

yoritaoshi: "force out and down" technique

yotsuzumo: style of sumo involving gripping the opponent's mawashi

yukata: Japanese-style dressing gown

yumitori-shiki: bow-twirling ceremony after the last makuuchi match

yusho: tournament championship

zabuton: cushion

zensho: all wins

zensho yusho: to win a championship undefeated (15–0)

Get your official Club Sumo Boy gear today!

T-shirts, key chains, postcards and other items, all featuring Mina Hall's famous Sumo Boy

For an official Sumo Boy catalog, contact Stone Bridge Press at **1-800-947-7271** or **sbp@stonebridge.com**.

Talk sumo on the World Wide Web!

Go to the Stone Bridge Press web site at **www.stonebridge.com**. From the home page, click on the sumo link to get to our sumo site. There you'll be able to contact author **Mina Hall** directly with questions about rikishi, rules, and anything else you want to know about sumo.

All questions and answers will be shared with other visitors on the Stone Bridge Press site. You'll also find the latest Sumo Boy items to add to your collection.

For further information about *The Big Book of Sumo* and other Stone Bridge Press publications, send e-mail to **sbp@stonebridge.com**, telephone toll-free **1-800-947-7271**, or write to **Stone Bridge Press, P.O. Box 8208, Berkeley, CA 94707**.